GEMMA LEVINE

PEOPLE

of

the

Text by
Sheridan Morley

In Aid of the Malcolm Sargent Cancer Fund for Children

90s

Foreword by
HRH The Princess of Wales

HarperCollins*Publishers*

For Ariella Rosie

I WOULD LIKE TO EXPRESS MY GRATITUDE TO:
Paul Winner, who introduced me to the Malcolm Sargent Cancer Fund for Children
Eddie Bell, my publisher, who received this publication with such enthusiasm
Juliet Van Oss, my editor
Lucy Allen, designer of the book
Pat Froomberg, my project advisor, who has guided me through the birth and development of twelve books
Lord King, who arranged my visit to Hong Kong so that Chris Patten could be included in this book
The Regent Hotel, Hong Kong, for their hospitality
Rob Carter, my invaluable assistant
Gordon, Nina, Donna, Lou, Chris and Richard of Gordon Bishop Associates, my black and white printing house
Hasselblad UK
Mike Shaw, my agent
Adele and Karen, who assisted with the diary
and finally all my sitters, who were gracious enough to give me approximately fifteen minutes of their
valuable time in the midst of their active schedules, and in particular Brian Keenan, Dublin.

A PERSONAL NOTE
. . . of sadness in the 90s with the death of my father, Ellis Josephs,
who died from cancer on 3 January 1991;
. . . of joy in the 90s with the birth of my first grandchild, Ariella Rosie Levine,
on 30 June 1992.

Gemma Levine

Hammersmith, London W6 8JB

Published by HarperCollins*Publishers* 1995
1 3 5 7 9 8 6 4 2

Copyright © 1995 Photographs
The Malcolm Sargent Cancer Fund for Children Limited

Copyright © 1995 Text Sheridan Morley

Gemma Levine and Sheridan Morley assert the moral right to
be identified as the photographer and author of this work

A catalogue record for this book
is available from the British Library

ISBN 0 00 255569 7

Set in Berkley Book

Printed in Great Britain by
HarperCollinsManufacturing Glasgow

THE TRUSTEES
OF THE MALCOLM SARGENT CANCER FUND FOR CHILDREN
WISH TO RECORD THEIR APPRECIATION TO

APV plc
Anheuser-Busch
British Airways plc
Enterprise Oil plc
The Publishers Association
The Morgan Crucible Company plc
News International plc
Glencore UK Ltd
The RTZ Corporation plc
White & Mackay Group plc

AND ESPECIALLY

Ronel Lehmann and staff
without whose efforts during the past three years
this book could not have been possible.

KENSINGTON PALACE

As Patron of The Malcolm Sargent Cancer Fund for Children, I am very glad that all royalties from the sales of this book will go to this special Charity. The Fund, which has played an essential part in the development of support to children with cancer, has helped over 17,000 children and their families since it was established in 1968.

We all hope and pray that our children will lead happy and healthy lives. But should cancer be diagnosed, the Fund helps tremendously to ease the many burdens on young people and their families.

The Fund relies on voluntary support. Through People of the 90s, you will be making a major contribution to its vital work.

Diana.

November, 1994

Her Royal Highness The Princess of Wales
Patron of the Malcolm Sargent Cancer Fund for Children

Sylvia Darley, OBE
Founder and Chief Executive, The Malcolm Sargent Cancer Fund for Children

INTRODUCTION

THIS BOOK is published in aid of the Malcolm Sargent Cancer Fund for Children to coincide with our celebrations for the centenary of the birth of Sir Malcolm Sargent in 1895, the brilliant pianist, organist and conductor in whose name the charity was established in 1968. Most readers will remember Sir Malcolm as Principal Conductor of the BBC Promenade Concerts. With the exception of Sir Henry Wood, no conductor has been more closely associated with 'The Proms'.

Harold Malcolm Watts Sargent was born in Ashford, Kent, the son of a coal merchant whose family has been connected with Stamford, Lincolnshire for some 400 years. During his early days he sang in his father's choir, learned to play the piano and took part in performances of Gilbert and Sullivan. At sixteen he was articled to the organist of Peterborough Cathedral, and at nineteen became organist of Melton Mowbray parish church. After a short spell in the army, he gained a Bachelor of Music from Durham, and later became the youngest Doctor of Music in the country. Within ten years he was associated with the Royal Choral Society and was conducting for the D'Oyly Carte Company, the Robert Mayer children's concerts and ballet performances for Diaghilev.

Sargent excelled in choral music direction and soon established a reputation with the great northern choirs. In 1934 he co-founded the London Philharmonic Orchestra with Sir Thomas Beecham, from 1939 until 1942 he was the Hallé's chief conductor, and in 1942 he revitalized the Liverpool Philharmonic Orchestra. He also became an accomplished broadcaster on BBC Radio. After the war Sargent became known as 'the Ambassador with the Baton' and appeared with the world's major orchestras. He was knighted in 1947, which was the first year he was invited to conduct at the Proms. In 1950 he succeeded Sir Adrian Bolt as the chief conductor of the BBC Symphony Orchestra – a post he held for seven years.

Sargent was much admired and adored by his Promenaders and concertgoers, many of whom remember him with affection to this day. When he died of cancer, the Promenaders approached me to set up the Malcolm Sargent Cancer Fund for Children in his memory.

The Fund is concerned with the welfare of all young people under the age of twenty-one who have any form of cancer, Hodgkin's disease or leukaemia. In the UK 1500 young people develop cancer every year. Although around seventy per cent will eventually be cured, treatment can be protracted and have unpleasant side effects. Families are disrupted, relationships suffer, brothers and sisters become resentful and pressures build up on parents.

The Fund receives no government support – its work depends upon private donations and fund-raising. Over 17,000 children and their families have received financial aid from the Fund since it started, and many more have received counselling from the ever-growing team of Malcolm Sargent social workers working alongside the hospital teams who care for and treat children. Nearly every main children's cancer treatment centre has at least one Malcolm Sargent social worker, and they are now also based in some of the smaller outlying centres.

In addition to the social workers, the Fund provides play therapists in Leeds, Inverness, Liverpool and Southampton, and a 'flying nurse' in the Highlands and Islands of Scotland. It also provides the only occupational therapist in the UK who works with children suffering from cancer. Two hundred children also go to Lake Windermere each August to enjoy the famous Malcolm Sargent Camp.

We provide grants for an enormous range of requests. A large proportion of money goes to parents to enable them to visit their child on a daily basis, and we help with heating bills (which are always high, as the children feel cold even in the summer), clothing, computers, toys and bedding. Grants are also made for hobbies, as these can provide great comfort to the child and the family at a time of enormous stress.

We have organized a number of special events and activities in 1995 to commemorate this special centenary year of Sir Malcolm and to raise the profile of the Fund. They include, notably, this marvellous book, an exhibition of photographs of all the sitters who kindly gave their time to Gemma Levine, and a magnificent charity gala birthday concert at the Royal Albert Hall. We hope that these and all our other activities will help raise the funds that are sorely needed to enable us to continue our crucial work for children with cancer.

Sylvia Darley

Sir Simon Rattle

The first British conductor in thirty years to achieve the superstar status of Bernstein or
Karajan, and the only man ever to have given Birmingham leading arts-centre status. His
CBSO is perennially underfunded and cash-strapped, but Rattle has renewed to 1997 and
remains oblivious to overseas offers despite increased guesting. Was knighted in 1994.

Juliet Stevenson

Truly, madly and deeply wonderful, she worked her way through a decade of RSC classics
(*As You Like It, Measure for Measure*), then went to the National for *Hedda* and the West
End for *Death and the Maiden*. Recently filmed David Hare's *Secret Rapture* and became a
one-parent mother; also went to Los Angeles for a fringe- theatre staging of *Scenes from an
Execution*. Hollywood calls are thus far unreturned, but not, I think, for long.

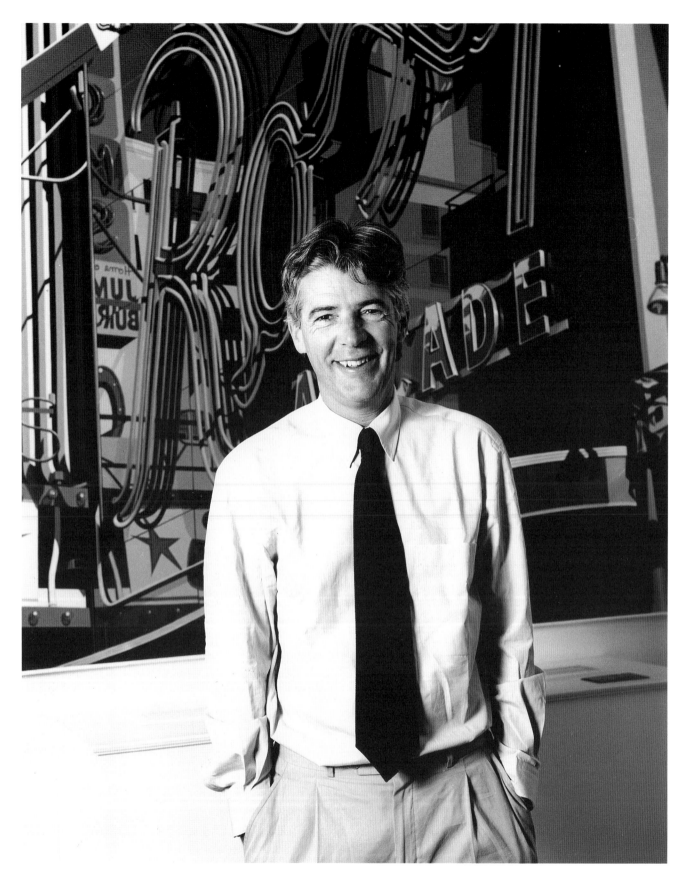

Michael Green

Head of Carlton Communications, he also chairs ITN, is the most powerful TV baron in the country, dislikes publicity and Rupert Murdoch, but gave the 1994 Royal Television Society lecture calling for more cross-ownership between broadcast and print media.

Shami Ahmed

Managing Director of the £30 million Joe Bloggs jeans empire. Started a corner shop at fourteen, but still thinks he didn't get into retail early enough. Recently sold a pair of diamond-encrusted denims for £100,000. 'You've got to be hungry.' Arrived in this country from Karachi aged two, and has lived in Manchester ever since.

Cardinal Basil Hume | Archbishop of Canterbury

Archbishop of Westminster since 1976 and therefore the nation's No. 1 Catholic. Spent forty years at Ampleforth as pupil then monk, teacher, housemaster and Abbot. Father was a Protestant. In 1976 Basil progressed from Abbot to Bishop to Archbishop to Cardinal in thirty-three days, reckoned to be the all-time record. Supports Newcastle United. Ladbroke's give him odds of 20–1 on being the next Pope.

George Carey, Archbishop since 1991, did National Service as an RAF wireless operator. Went to secondary modern school in Barking before King's College London; married with two sons and two daughters. Was a surprise choice to be the 103rd Archbishop: odds were 23–1 against him. Controversially announced that 'social deprivation' was the cause of the Tyneside riots. Thinks that 'Morality has now been privatized.'

Sir Ian MacLaurin

Chairman of Tesco and a prominent member of the MCC. Born in Blackheath in 1937. Also a director of Guinness and the NatWest. Reckons he has another three or four years before he reaches his sell-by date. Took a pay-cut of £200,000 in 1993 but that still left him £794,000 for the year. Don't mention Safeways.

Norma Major

Wrote an excellent biography of Joan Sutherland.
Married John. Queued at Wembley for Torvill & Dean even when First Lady.
'Everything John has ever done has been a bed of nails.'

Nick Faldo

The world's leading golfer, he beat Nicklaus in the Ryder Cup when he was twenty, and that was seventeen years ago. Married (and divorced) a journalist who came to interview him; has seldom talked to the press since. Reckoned to earn £134 for every swing of his club. Likes fly fishing. Three times winner of the French Open among many others.

Sally Gunnell

The first woman in history to complete the Grand Slam of Athletics titles – Commonwealth, World, Olympics and European 400 metres. Parents farm 300 acres of Essex, husband is her manager. Averages £10,000 a race plus sponsorships, plans to retire after the next Olympics and start a family. Her autobiography is entitled *Running Tall*.

Gary Rhodes

Uncharitably described as 'the Nigel Kennedy of *haute cuisine*', television's latest star chef is based at the Greenhouse in Mayfair. Made his reputation on all-British dishes: he still does the best treacle sponge, and his mum does the steak and kidney. Once wanted to be a police dog handler – Gary, that is, not his mum. Has just taken over catering at the Festival Hall, which is good news for concertgoers.

Damien Hirst

Carver of dead cows and pickler of sheep, Britain's most controversial artist now designs opera
sets. Once entered an eighteen-foot shark in a tank of formaldehyde for the Turner Prize. Charles
Saatchi paid £50,000 for it. Educated in Leeds, failed at St Martin's, wants to be John Lennon.
Art critic Brian Sewell thinks 'he needs his bottom smacked'.

Fiona Shaw

Played Electra, Hedda and Brecht's *Good Woman of Setzuan* with primal and ferocious power; also does manic villainesses in Hollywood action adventures. *The Times* reckons her the most feral actress alive: 'Her nerves stand out in a refreshingly un-English way.' She also spearheads the new Irish invasion of theatre and cinema worldwide.

Martin Taylor

Chief Executive of Barclays Bank, he started out as a financial journalist. The youngest-ever leader of a major clearing bank, he was appointed at forty-one in 1993 just in time to face small-business objections to the profits declared in an era of recession and overdraft cutbacks. Studied Chinese at Oxford, thinks that banks are meant to be businesses rather than charities, and believes that computers make fewer bad loan decisions than old-style human managers.

Tony Blair

The man most likely to be the next prime minister. Father-in-law starred in 'Till Death Us Do Part'. His honeymoon-period promises included support from Marks & Spencer, maybe even from Rupert Murdoch. Unkind observers remark that, had the Labour Party elected the late Kim Il Sung as their leader in 1994, he too would now be in with a chance for 1996-7. Luckily we got Bambi instead.

Rabbi Julia Neuberger

At forty-four, she is the first woman rabbi in the world to have her own congregation. Teaches rabbinical students at Leo Baeck College. Father was a civil servant, mother a Jewish refugee. Hopes after death to rot and produce wonderful rose trees. On the 1994 Booker jury; took understandable objection to the voting procedures. Chairman of Camden and Islington NHS Trust since 1983.

Peter Carter-Ruck

Britain's most celebrated libel lawyer, still on the case at eighty. Much feared by journalists, though he reckons he
has defended newspapers far more often than their plaintiffs. Married for fifty-two years to Pamela, with whom he
has restored a crofter's cottage in the Western Highlands. Likes Bizet, Cole Porter and 'Question Time' on BBC1;
also very fond of *Casablanca* (the film, not the city) and the Impressionists.

Nigel Short

First appeared on 'Blue Peter' as a bespectacled adolescent boffin playing the bass for
his school band. Latterly more famous for having lost the World Chess Championship
and £1 million to Gary Kasparov. Still the British Grandmaster. 'Chess is just a contest:
you win some, lose some.'

Terry Waite

Former Special Envoy to the Archbishop of Canterbury and possibly an unwitting dupe
of the CIA. Taken hostage in January 1987. Now lives in Suffolk and has written a book
about solitude. After 1763 days in mostly solitary confinement, he should know.

Gail Rebuck

Chairman and Chief Executive of Random House, she is rumoured to have given one of her daughters
an office as a sixth-birthday present. Not so much loved by the old Bloomsbury set, but reckoned to have
inherited Carmen Callil's role as the 'glass ceiling-breaker' for women in publishing, though they still only make
up sixty per cent of the workforce and barely twenty per cent of the directors. '5 foot 9 of feminine charm and
commercial acumen,' thought *The Times*. Quick responses, power breakfasts, the American approach.

Nigel Hawthorne

Forever the ruthlessly urbane Sir Humphrey of 'Yes Minister' and 'Yes, Prime Minister', Hawthorne denies all similarities. Arriving in London in 1951 with £12, he spent several fruitless years in search of agents and jobs, 'smelling of failure'. Joan Littlewood at Stratford East turned his career around, and since then has come the stage *Shadowlands*, long RSC and National seasons and Alan Bennett's *Madness of George III,* which he is now filming.

Baroness O'Cathain

Controversial but dynamic Managing Director of the Barbican Centre from January 1990 until November 1994 when she departed amid considerable acrimony. The liberal arts establishment had instantly branded her 'dangerously Thatcherite'. Nevertheless, she managed to improve the foyers, upgrade the bars and bookshops, and hold the fort against vociferous opposition.

Anthony Michaels Moore

Since joining the Royal Opera in 1987, he has rapidly come to recognition as one of
the world's leading lyric baritones, singing with all the major opera houses, orchestras and
conductors. In 1993 he made his debuts with La Scala and the Vienna Philharmonic; last
year he performed in Turin and at the Opéra de la Bastille in Paris. Is a former schoolmaster.

Helen Sharman

Britain's first astronaut, she trained for the Anglo-Soviet Juno mission in 1991. Now a satellite consultant, but still known as 'The Girl from Mars', not because she got there but because she once worked in the chocolate factory. That was where she read an ad, 'Astronaut Wanted'. Simple, really.

Win Bischoff

Educated in South Africa, built up Schroders Asia in Hong Kong, returned to London a decade ago to become Chairman of J. Henry Schroder Wagg and a few months later Group Chief Executive of Schroders. Likes opera, skiing and golf.

Greg Hutchings

Earned £1 million in 1991-2 as Chief Executive of Tomkins (who sell everything from lawnmowers to handguns). Recently paid £1 billion for Ranks Hovis McDougall, but the flour power refuses to push shares much above 230p. Hutchings reckons it'll prove self-raising soon enough.

Baroness Thatcher

We are an ex-prime minister. We are sixty-nine and still available, should the call come. Never forget that General de Gaulle was a lot older when they brought him back from Colombey les Deux Églises.

Dr Jonathan Sacks

Chief Rabbi since 1991. Double first in Philosophy at Cambridge, started teaching at Jews' College in 1971, ordained himself in 1976, became Rabbi of Golder's Green and then Marble Arch synagogues. Promises a decade of renewal at a time when one in three Jews marries outside the faith and the numbers of the Orthodox have declined by a third since World War Two to 300,000 in Britain. Married with three children; refused in 1992 to allow women-only rabbis at Stanmore, or to have men and women sit together in the synagogue.

John Birt | Eve Pollard

Director-General of the BBC, which he joined in 1987 from ITV. 'I was seen as the alien from commerce, rather as though a Protestant had suddenly become Pope.' Now, after some controversial months involving his contractual arrangements and designer suiting, he is generally credited with safeguarding the BBC licence fee and ensuring its survival beyond the millennium. Defining its aims as 'doing what market-driven commercial TV never can', he speaks up for everything from children's broadcasting to 'doing justice to the national canon of drama and literature'. Auntie may yet grow fond of her renegade nephew.

Editor of the *Sunday Express* 1991-4, before that edited the *Sunday Mirror* and *You* Magazine. Launched *Elle* USA and fights splendidly for women in journalism. One of the few to have made it to the top there.

Peggy Czyzak-Dannenbaum

And that's just her name: she's a specialist hand-craft baker, supplying major chain stores with all kinds of daily bread; almost single-handed, she brought ciabatta bread to Britain, and where would we be without that now? She's also a demon foot-baller, runs La Fornaia, which is one of the most successful small companies in the UK (so says London Business School between mouthfuls) and hails from Massachusetts where she went to college with Hillary Clinton. La Fornaia turned over £5 billion's worth of bread in 1992–3.

Brian Lara

The most charismatic cricketer since Don Bradman, a gentle Trinidadian who in April 1994 achieved the highest test score in history: 375 for the West Indies against England. Known as the Prince, aged twenty-five, he made £500,000 in fees and journalism and sponsorship last year. He is not thought to keep gardening soil in his trouser pockets. Trinidad has just given him a free building plot.

Eddie Mirzoeff | John Major

Made the 'Elizabeth R' documentary in 1991 after a long and distinguished BBC career as Executive Producer BBC Documentaries. Also made all the best of the 'Real Lives' and John Betjeman documentaries. Was made a Commander of the Royal Victorian Order for monarchical services. Likes visiting Italy, walking in Wiltshire and exploring the London Library.

Born in 1943, the Year of the Goat in Chinese mythology. The first post-Thatcher PM, he established a Trollope memorial in Westminster Abbey, and hoped for a classless society, which suggests a somewhat tenuous grasp of Britain in the mid-90s.

The Corneal Laser Team

Together this remarkable team (*left to right*: Hari Adhikary, Terry Ramsell, Bernard Garston, Christopher Neave, Jitendra Tolia) established Britain's first specialist excimer laser facility at Clatterbridge Hospital on Merseyside in 1991. Through their pioneering work, people for the first time could experience life without dependence on spectacles or contact lenses. In the four years since they started, the team has operated on five thousand patients suffering from eye disease, working on the cornea without the need for a general anaesthetic. Laser clinics in their image are now opening all over Britain.

Jonny and Greg Searle and Gary Herbert

The brothers and their cox set two targets in 1992 – to win the Olympic trials in April and the final in August. They achieved both, despite a hair-raising loss of five strokes at the start of the final. On now to Atlanta 96. Gary is the first cox, meanwhile, to get an MBE for services to rowing.

Reverend Ulla Stefan Monberg

One of the first women to be ordained priest in the Church of England. Daughter of a prominent Copenhagen barrister, she trained for the priesthood at Cambridge, and was Curate of St James's Piccadilly 1990–94. Is at present Dean of Women's Ministry and Area Director of Ordinands in the Diocese of London; has campaigned widely for women's ordination at home and abroad.

Georgina Von Etzdorf

The leader of fashion's velvet underground, much worn by The Princess of Wales, Charlotte Rampling et al. Daughter of a Prussian father and English mother, she aims to run 'the best surface and colour company in Europe ... The idea is that when you take your eye off the pattern it moves on.' She and two other Camberwell art students formed her company in 1980. Estimated current turnover £2 million.

Kenneth Clarke | Paul Dacre

Chancellor of the Exchequer, the middle manager from middle England, last of the Heathmen in cabinet, hailed by the *Daily Express* as 'an overweight, fun-loving, self-confessed drinker, cigar smoker and jazz fan'. Just as long as he sticks with the tax cuts: The *Daily Mail* thinks he may be a secret socialist.

Editor of the *Daily Mail* since 1992; before that, the *Evening Standard*. Father was on the *Sunday Express*. Read English at Leeds, reported (like his Chairman, Sir David English) with distinction from New York for several seasons, dislikes 'the liberal consensus which has undermined the family and a belief in right and wrong'. Circulation approaching two million. Reckons TV has nearly had it as an advertising medium: 'The remote-control zapper has killed it.'

Irek Mukhamedov | Les Ferdinand

Once the glory of the Bolshoi, now the hottest ticket at the Royal Ballet, which he joined in 1990 after fleeing Moscow. Reckoned to be the natural successor to Nureyev, he fled when his dancer wife was first pregnant and they realized they wanted to bring up a family in the West. Since Sir Kenneth MacMillan's death, the rumours are that he might develop his own company over here for new work.

A striker rated £4 million (that was the Arsenal bid), who was kept out of the World Cup by injury but should be available for the next. A Notting Hill painter and decorator before the soccer scouts found him, he spent a year on loan to Turkey where he was surprised to find that they started the season by slaughtering a sheep and dabbing its blood on players. Fans would also stone them for such offences as a goalless away draw. Hasn't been back since.

Ronald Cohen | Peter Stothard

Founder/Chairman of Apax Partners and therefore one of this country's leading venture capitalists. Former President of the Oxford Union, moved into equity banking in France and later founded with others the City Group for Smaller Companies. Don't phone him for a cheaper mortgage, but most other financial queries gracefully received.

Became editor of *The Times* at forty in 1992. Started with the BBC and the National Theatre, but has been with *The Times* for fifteen years, principally in America. Thinks the present government is 'an unravelling piece of knitting', and would be surprised if Major fought the next election. Doesn't rule out *Times* support for Tony Blair, nor does his proprietor. Meanwhile he has initiated a price-cutting war which has altered the trade more radically than anything in the decade since the move to Wapping.

Richard Charkin

Chief Executive of Reed International Books. Born 1949 in London, educated at Cambridge and Harvard, came up through Harrap and Pergamon before joing the OUP and then Reed in 1988. Former captain of Baldons Cricket Club. What did you expect, an unflattering photograph?

Sir Terence Conran

Design guru, restaurateur and former husband of the best-selling Shirley, this is the man who has given us Habitat, the Design Museum, the Neal Street Restaurant, Bibendum, Quaglino's and the Butler's Wharf gastro-centre. He now promises a thousand-seat restaurant, bakery, bar and café on the old Marquee site in Soho. Asked once if he ever read trashy blockbusters, he said only when Shirley sent them to him.

Michael Dobbs

Author of the compellingly cynical *House of Cards* and *To Play the King*, now Tory party Deputy Chairman, not the first bestseller in that office – the last was Jeffrey Archer. A rather better writer, though? You might think so; I couldn't possibly comment.

Graham Kirkham

Founded the family furniture business in 1969 with just £100. By 1993 it was Britain's leading upholstered furniture specialist with a public value of £300 million. The son of a Yorkshire miner, Kirkham is a grammar schoolboy made very good indeed; still works seven days a week, but finds time to collect Impressionist masterpieces, among them the Manet *Bar at the Folies-Bergères*.

Richard Branson | Olga Polizzi

Airline owner, record salesman, daredevil transatlantic pilot, entrepreneur extraordinaire, charity fundraiser. Estimated net worth £895 million. Opens the first New York Virgin Megastore in Times Square in 1995. Is in partnership with the Japanese to develop London's Thameside County Hall as a hotel. Plans to run passenger trains through the Chunnel to Brussels. 'I've tried to do things differently, and that makes life more enjoyable.' British Airways might disagree.

Eldest daughter of Lord Forte, now runs the Building and Design division of her father's hotel empire, responsible for the design and refurbishment of eight hundred hotels worldwide with a budget of over £100 million a year. Married to author William Shawcross, she got the CBE in Thatcher's resignation honours and is co-Chairman of the Grosvenor House Art and Antiques Fair.

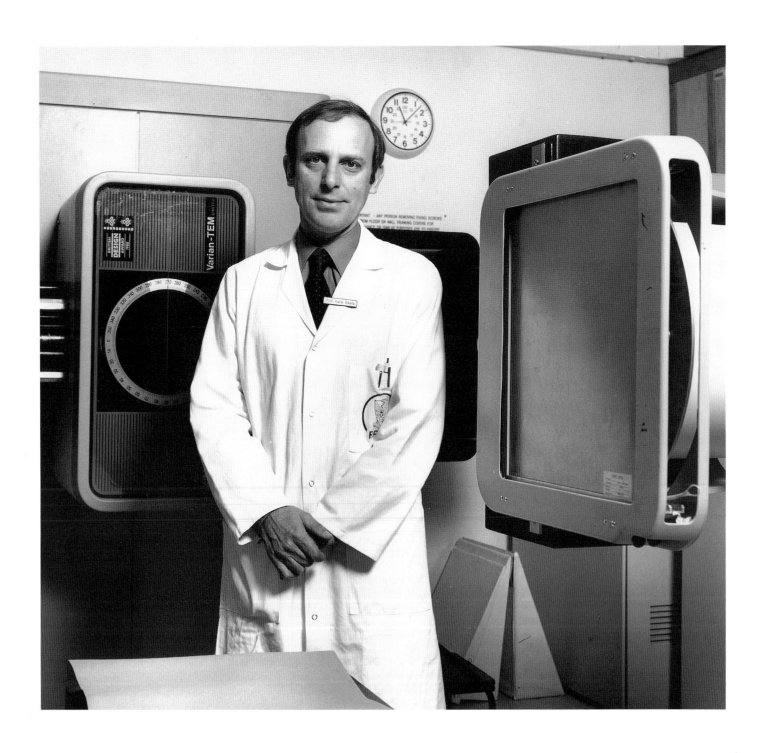

Professor Karol Sikora

Professor of Clinical Oncology at Hammersmith Hospital since 1986, specialist in
Cancer and Gene Therapy: '5000 people die unnecessarily of cancer in this country:
services are badly organized, understaffed and underfunded. Patients have a worse
chance here than in India.'

Dr Marsha Y Morgan

Senior Lecturer in Medicine and an Honorary Consultant Physician at the Royal Free in London: special interest in alcohol-related liver disease and alcohol abuse, on which she advises the Ministry of Transport driving panel. One of the leading members of the Government Working Party on Women and Alcohol: not one with whom to query the validity of the Breathalyzer.

Brian Keenan

Won the Irish Literature Prize for *An Evil Cradling*, considered by some to be the best of all the hostage books.
Was four years in captivity, on what he now calls his holidays. 'I refuse to get morbid about it. I learnt too much
while I was there.' In his book he thanks Islamic Jihad, 'without whom it could never have been written'.

John McCarthy and Jill Morrell

The love story of the 90s: a very British hero and the girl who campaigned for his release. Their joint memoirs have sold half a million in hardback. They have commendably refused to be the hostage answer to Torvill & Dean.

Elizabeth Esteve-Coll

Director of the V&A, she was accused of Thatcherism and 'vulgar popularism' when several
of her curators were made redundant. Married a Spanish sea captain and Franco refugee who
was thirty years her senior; since his death has survived internecine warfare at the V&A as it
struggles to come into the present while still celebrating the past.

Peter Scudamore

Former jump jockey and eight times world champion who in 1993 beat a time-trial record over 200 miles which had stood for nearly two centuries. In a fifteen-year career, Scudamore rode more than sixteen hundred winners – another record.

Pat Eddery

Champion royal jockey, he has been riding winners for the Queen for a full quarter-century
and seems a likely starter for the Piggott stakes. 'All a jockey needs is the drive and the will to
win.' Father, grandfather and five brothers were and are also jockeys.

Paddy Ashdown

Leader of the Liberal Democrats, a post requiring tenacity mixed with optimism. Has
survived a private-life crisis, but now has to face defection of the Gang of Three to Blair, plus
poor showings in Euro-elections. On the other hand, polls point out that he's still a
lot more popular than the PM. Likes gardening and wine-making.

Michael Portillo | Alison Wilding

Employment Secretary, Heseltine-in-waiting, he could well be the focus for the anti-Majorites. Speaks up for the 'still small voice of Britain's quiet majority' in a somewhat louder one. Middle names are Denzil Xavier. Brazilian finance minister thinks 'his ambition may be superior to his intelligence'.

Once shortlisted for the Turner Prize, she is one of the best-known female sculptors in Britain. Makes light of heavy metal. Eager to avoid novelty and shock effects, she has been hailed for 'making stone and copper seem like entirely new and precious artifacts, unearthed by her sensitive feeling for materials and a human interest that doesn't need spelling out'.

Joan Bakewell

Amazingly now a grandmother in her early sixties, she has never escaped Frank Muir's
epithet 'the thinking man's crumpet'. Truth is she was the first woman to make the arts
interesting and respectable on late-night television, the first to suggest she'd been hired for
a brain rather than a body, the first to pioneer the forty-minute, live, face-to-face interview.
I should know, I was there with her for seven years on 'Late Night Line-Up' from 1966.
She now fronts 'Heart of the Matter' on BBC1.

Judge Stephen Tumim

Circuit Judge and HM Chief Inspector of Prisons since 1987. Described by the *Guardian*
as 'Pickwick at the Garrick'. Father was a clerk of assize at Oxford, where the Judge took a
history degree before 'drifting into the law out of laziness'. Has since campaigned for better
conditions in Holloway, Strangeways and Brixton among other overcrowded Victorian prisons.
Collects second-hand books and frequently reviews more recent ones, especially on the
law and penal reform.

Eddie George | Chris Patten

The first Governor of the Bank of England ever to like being called Eddie. Joined straight from Cambridge in 1962. Became known as Steady Eddie for getting the bank through its 300th anniversary in 1994. 'We have taken a bit of a battering, but we are still in there, troops intact.' After 300 years, what's an occasional Black Wednesday?

Our man in charge of handing back Hong Kong to the Chinese on 1st July 1997. Son of a music publisher, he read history at Oxford. May retreat from Hong Kong before the Chinese get there. In that event, he will still be young enough (fifty-three) to succeed Major or to go to the UN, World Bank, European Commission etc.

Felicity Kendal

Gorgeous British television sitcom star who, like her original 'Good Life' partners (Briers, Eddington and Keith), has managed the transition to a serious stage career. A child actress who toured India with her parents (first appeared on stage at nine months in *A Midsummer Night's Dream*), twice married, often now linked to Tom Stoppard, she is one of our best high-comedy stylists for all media. Plays golf.

Maggie Koumi

Editor of *Hello!* magazine. Lives in the same Covent Garden flat where she was born in July 1942 of Greek parentage. Began her career at fifteen as a secretary in Thomas Cook's head office, graduating from there to magazines such as *Boyfriend*, *Top Boys Fortnightly*, *Big Beat Monthly* and *Boyfriend Annual*, then became Editor of *19* for seventeen years. Was approached in 1987 by the Spanish proprietors of *Hola!* to work on an English dummy, which appeared as *Hello!* in May 1988. Was appointed co-editor, becoming sole editor in 1993. The magazine has achieved a readership of just over two million. Has been married since 1980 to a Barcelona artist.

Anthony Scrivener, QC

Recorder of the Crown Court since 1976, called to the Bar in 1958, went out to Ghana as a lecturer in law. Likes tennis, chess and racing cars. Was Chairman of the Bar Council in 1991.

Sir Bryan Carsberg

Director General of Fair Trading since 1992. Likes road-running, theatre and classical music. Started out as a chartered accountant: author of *An Introduction to Mathematical Programming for Accountants* and *The Evaluation of Financial Performance in the Water Industry*, bestsellers both. Has successfully killed off the Net Book Agreement; later clashed with the British film industry over its right to decide which cinemas should show films and for how long. Supporters of his years at Oftel said, 'Carsberg – the best managing director in the world.' A lager joke.

Lord King

Pugnacious President of British Airways, where he was Chairman 1981-93. Lady Thatcher's favourite businessman, though probably not Richard Branson's. Originally made fame and fortune manufacturing ball bearings. Don't ask about Virgin territory; fly the flag.

Charles Saumarez Smith

Educated at Marlborough, Cambridge and Harvard, was an assistant keeper and Head of Research at the V&A, now runs the National Portrait Gallery. Wrote the definitive study of the Building of Castle Howard, is an expert on eighteenth-century decoration, joined the NPG in time for its triumphant Sitwell exhibition, now continues in enviable charge of portraits, photographs and of course portrait photographs on and off the Beaton track.

Michael Grade

Scion of the most successful dynasty in all British showbiz since the war, he now heads
Channel 4. Before that, BBC1 and light entertainment at LWT. Three cigars a day, red braces, one
of the last of the old-style showmen, he regularly lays into the BBC, 'a kingdom of fear'. He is
currently trying to devolve Channel 4 from ITV and achieve full economic independence.

Timberlake Wertenbaker

Overheard at the Royal Court: 'I once went to school with a Timberlake Wertenbaker; I wonder if it could be the same one?' On balance, it probably is. The leading female dramatist of her generation (*Our Country's Good*, about an early penal colony in rehearsal in Sydney 200 years ago; *Three Birds Alighting on a Field*, about the money-sexy-social resident in London), she has long been resident in London, a quintessentially theatrical writer with no desire to go home. 'New York has to be seduced all the time; here they just let you work.'

Derek Wanless

Made Chief Executive of the NatWest at forty-four, he claims it to be Britain's
Greenest bank. Joined from Cambridge with a first in, reassuringly, mathematics.
Has seen the bank through its Blue Arrow crisis and back on target.

Alan Yentob

Controller of BBC1, before that BBC2, and briefly both in tandem. Wants 'a channel of conviction, offering surprise in a culture of reprise'. Originally a Music & Arts man, he has adapted well to the wider demands of the main entertainment channel. Read law at Leeds, closed 'Eldorado', lives with TV director Philippa Walker, has two children.

Esther Rantzen

Hosted 'That's Life' for twenty-one years, giving British TV a unique mix of vaudeville
and consumerism on a weekly basis, rather as though Ken Dodd in drag had been a Samaritan.
Now back as our very own Oprah in a new TV chat show. Known as the nation's nanny,
but has done valuable work for Childline.

Susan Crosland

Baltimore-born journalist and now novelist who wrote an infinitely touching biography of her husband Anthony, who died of a heart attack in 1977 after a distinguished Cabinet life as Foreign Secretary. Her latest novel concerns a journalist who is unexpectedly appointed ambassador to Washington and ends up as aide to a ruthless tycoon. Those who see it as a closet biography of Peter Jay have been firmly disillusioned by the author.

Bruno Rotti

Career began at the age of six when he helped his parents run a small private club in Italy; later moved to Turin, worked for twenty-five years at Claridge's, and now manages Mark's Club in Charles Street. A face well known to anyone who eats smartly in London.

Lord Gowrie

Arts Council Chairman and former Tory Arts Minister who famously resigned in 1985 because he couldn't survive on £33,000 a year. Better paid now by Sotheby's, and generally thought to be a wise choice for the Council, he has become something of an Establishment figure. Didn't care for Vikram Seth's *A Suitable Boy* when he was chairing the Booker panel, and offered to edit it down a bit. 'May God and literature forgive you,' responded the prizewinning author.

Policewoman Karen Greene

David Suchet | John Suchet

Son of a Harley Street specialist, brother of John, he has spent most of the 90s as BBC TV's Hercule Poirot, though his stage work is considerably more varied: a memorable RSC Iago and Shylock, Mamet's *Oleanna,* and a play about Sid Field. Napoleon and Rasputin are still on his hitlist of desirable roles.

Newscaster who famously advised brother David never to play Hercule Poirot on television. Educated at Uppingham and St Andrews, started at Reuters, TV journalist of the year 1986.

Sir Colin Marshall

Chairman of British Airways since Exit the King. His own tips include flying Concorde wherever possible, taking work with you on the flight rather than trying to finish it in the office before take-off, travelling with a clean shirt, and staying in the best hotel available on arrival. Salary for 1993 was quoted at £788,000. Don't ask, 'Are you on standby too?'

Piers Morgan

Appointed Editor of the *News of the World* in 1994 at twenty-nine, the youngest national editor for more than half a century. Before that he wrote the pop column for the *Sun*, which can also claim two other future editors: John Blake of the *People* and Martin Dunn of the *NY Daily News*.

Sir Paul Condon | Zoë Wanamaker

Commissioner of the Metropolitan Police since 1992, left school at sixteen, started on the beat in Bethnal Green, has decided that police must now carry firearms in potential troublespots. Youngest-ever Commissioner, politically correct rather than 'hang 'em and flog 'em'; believes there should be more black and homosexual officers.

The sexually magnetic star of 'Love Hurts', she is now fulfilling the dream of her father Sam to recreate Shakespeare's Globe on its original South Bank site. Recent stage work includes *Dead Funny* (which was) and Miller's *The Last Yankee*. Has lived here all her life, is fed up with people asking whether she feels American and why she hasn't married, also dislikes the Hollywood habit of giving all the best roles only to golden blondes.

Tony Bevan | David Hockney

Compared to Lucien Freud and Stanley Spencer, often favourably, this graduate of Goldsmiths' and the Slade is a painter of anti-portraits often reckoned to have declared war on the Royal Society of Portrait Painters. The *Guardian* thinks him the finest figurative painter of his generation. Has a bleak, spiky style. Aged forty-four, born in Bradford.

Arguably Britain's greatest living artist, he has long been self-exiled to California, where the primary colours of electric-blue swimming pools and skies have defined a style which he has since applied to Fax-Art, computer and laser prints. Peter Pan meets W.H. Auden as the boy from Bradford and Covent Garden Opera faces up to his mid-fifties. 'I'm deeply aware that my world is full of sadness, not least the Aids deaths of two dozen good friends. But the urge to pleasure is still strong – I try to express my own joy in the world, no matter how bad it is.'

Rocco Forte | Sir Richard Greenbury

Born Bournemouth in 1945, only son of Lord Forte, now succeeds him as Chairman of Forte plc. Educated at Oxford, studied accountancy, became a director of Forte in 1973. Pioneered the Travelodge division and spearheaded the ongoing fight for the Savoy. Married with a son and two daughters, he also runs marathons.

Chairman of Marks & Spencer since 1991, having worked there for forty-two of his fifty-eight years, starting at £4 a week on the shop floor at Ealing after his parents' divorce. Spends his weekends in M&S stores. 'We have 14 million customers – they tell me whether we are getting it right or wrong.' Yes, some stores do now reluctantly open on Sundays. Has decided to invest in Tony Blair among other political donations.

Joanna Trollope

Fifth-generation niece of Anthony Trollope, daughter of a Gloucestershire rector, she spent two years in the Foreign Office before turning to what are now known as her 'Aga sagas'. Has also written, pseudonymously, a series of historical novels. Best known Aga saga: *The Rector's Wife* (starring Lindsay Duncan on TV). Still writes in longhand; wanted to be a painter. 'I have no moral horsewhips to crack – life is so difficult and complicated we must all struggle through as best we can.'

Lord McAlpine

Multimillionaire construction chief who once described himself as 'Mrs Thatcher's Bagman' – officially Tory Party Treasurer 1975-90. Author of *The Servant*, a Machiavellian update about power politics and how to survive them. Known at Stowe as Roly Poly, he left with three O levels. Lives near Venice, is writing a political novel. Jovial reactionary with a stunning collection of Australian aboriginal art.

Deborah Warner

Recently in conflict with Glyndebourne die-hards over *Don Giovanni* and the Samuel Beckett
estate over minor alterations to his stage directions. Before that, award-winning revivals of
A Doll's House and *Electra* and the stunning *Hedda* with Fiona Shaw. The RSC relies on her for
the 'unpopulars' (*Titus Andronicus*, *King John*). Started as a stage manager. Reckons a university
degree is even more of a handicap than being female in the theatre.

William Boyd

Won the Whitbread for *A Good Man in Africa* in 1981, the Somerset Maugham a year later and £20,000 from the *Sunday Express* for *The Blue Afternoon* in 1993. Started out as a teacher at a girls' public school, then moved to St Hilda's in Oxford. Novels since then include *Brazzaville Beach* and *An Ice Cream War*. Lacks the urban angst of other leading contemporaries. 'I'm just very lucky to be able to earn my living writing novels.'

Virginia Bottomley

Arguably the most unpopular politician of recent times, and that is some contest. Secretary of State for Health, widely credited with dismantling the NHS and some of its better teaching hospitals. 'An aroma of merciless do-gooding,' says an observer in the *Observer*. Maybe it's just her fabulous ability to be misunderstood.

John Ritblat

Chairman of British Land, which doubled pretax profits to £54 million in 1994. Son of a Hampstead dentist, he foresaw the revival of the London property market, and is now reckoned to be one of the shrewdest rent collectors in the City.

Darcey Bussell

The Royal Ballet's youngest and most popular prima ballerina. Hailed as the new Fonteyn, she is reckoned by *The Times* to have the best legs in London and by the *Telegraph* to have danced in *Sleeping Beauty* as 'an Aurora for this generation to cherish'. Still not twenty-six, she became a soloist at nineteen after the late Sir Kenneth MacMillan plucked her from the corps de ballet for his *Prince of the Pagodas*.

Matthew Hart

First Artist with the Royal Ballet who in 1988, when only sixteen, began to win the dance awards that now crowd his bookcase. He frequently dances his own work as a choreographer, and has made works for Dance Umbrella as well as the Royal Ballet School. His first professional commission, *Street*, was premiered by Birmingham Royal Ballet in June 1993; later came *Fanfare* for the Royal Opera House and *Caught Dance*. He has danced the title role in Ninette de Valois' *The Rake's Progress*, and in 1992–3 made his debut as Bratfisch in Kenneth MacMillan's *Mayerling*, the Jester in Frederick Ashton's *Cinderella* and Squirrel Nutkin in *Tales of Beatrix Potter*.

Jung Chang | Lorraine Pascale

Once a Red Guard, she is the author of *Wild Swans* which, after fifty weeks on the bestseller lists, returned to first place with a million copies sold. Robert Bolt is doing the TV serialization of this complex story of three women from feudal times to the end of the Cultural Revolution. Opening line: 'At fifteen, my grandmother became the concubine of a warlord.' Best line: 'My school was founded in 141 BC.' She is now working on the biography of Mao Tse-tung with her husband, the Far East scholar Jon Halliday.

The first black model ever to appear on the cover of American *Elle*. Grew up in Devon, was spotted on the street in her teens, made her name in the Haagen-Dazs commercials, has recently worked for Benetton and The Gap. Did nine fashion shows in Paris and eighteen in New York in 1994 alone.

David Sainsbury

Reckoned to be the second-wealthiest Briton, with almost £2 billion in his personal account. Born 1940, Chief Executive of the family supermarkets, he is often described as resembling an Israeli army general in mufti. Lives modestly, and gives vast charitable donations to African development programmes, healthcare and disadvantaged children. Studied psychology at Cambridge. Reckons the British have never properly appreciated veal.

Michael Rasser

The Michael of Michaeljohn hairdressing. Studied in London, went to work for Revlon in New York, toured as Judy Garland's hairdresser. Came back to London in time for the Swinging Sixties: styled for David Bailey shoots, notably with Twiggy on her very first photographic assignment. Michael now runs the London operation while John Isaacs looks after the California branch.

Terry Maher

Founder of Pentos (which owns Dillon's Bookstores), the bookselling chain he built from a £100 company into a £250 million business before leaving in 1993. A firm opponent of retail price maintenance on books; has published his autobiography, *Against My Better Judgement*; is currently developing a number of new interests within the trade.

Dame Elizabeth Butler-Sloss

The nation's top woman judge, who after years of being officially called Lord Justice Butler-Sloss, despite her success, won in 1994 the right to be declared Lady Justice Butler-Sloss. First woman to arrive on the Appeal Court bench; she also headed the Cleveland child abuse enquiry in 1988. Husband was a High Court judge in Kenya. Two sons, one daughter also a partner in a law firm; sons are theatrical producers and critics.

Eddie Bell

Chairman and Publisher of HarperCollins. What did you expect, an unflattering photograph?
Born 1949, started with Hodder & Stoughton, then Collins. Launched Harper Paperbacks in
America. Supports Arsenal, collects old books, sells new ones.

Jenni Murray

Chief 'Woman's Hour' presenter since 1987. Born in Barnsley, the only child of an
engineer, she started out hoping to be an actress. Worried older Radio 4 listeners by
announcing that 'Marriage is an insult and women shouldn't touch it'. Lives in
Battersea with an ex-submariner and their two children.

Lord Taylor of Gosforth

Lord Chief Justice since 1992. Born 1930, son of a doctor, educated in Newcastle-upon-Tyne and at Cambridge. Called to the Bar in 1954 to the Inner Temple. Opposed the Lord Chancellor on the reform of the magistrates' courts because he thought they would undermine judicial independence. Also strongly opposed the Home Secretary's proposal to curb a suspect's right to remain silent at trial. Successfully challenged the Government on the 1991 Criminal Justice Act, forcing a U-turn on sentencing procedures.

Christopher Corbin and Jeremy King

These two took two of the oldest-established luvvie eateries in the West End, The Ivy and Le Caprice, and turned them into modern smash hits that are still theatrical but without the red-velvet plushery. Instead they are minimalist cool. If you want to eat well and late in London stay close to them, except maybe when they are on their motorbikes commuting between Arlington and West Streets.

Andrew Neil

Editor of the *Sunday Times* for a decade, he then went on long leave to start up a TV newsmagazine for Murdoch's American Fox network. Described as 'the intellectual exocet from Paisley', he edited the London section of *The Economist* before replacing Frank Giles, who became Editor Emeritus ('E means you're out and Meritus means you deserve it' - attrib. R Murdoch). Neil was to get half a million pounds for six months on American TV, and some thought he would have liked to stay there; British journalism would have been quieter and poorer, whatever Peregrine Worsthorne tells you.

Sir Anthony Hopkins

The greatest Welsh actor/film star since Richard Burton, of whom he can do a stunning impression. Winner of two Oscars for *Silence of the Lambs* and *Remains of the Day* (a prize always denied Burton himself), Hopkins emerged from the wreckage of a midlife crisis to build a Hollywood career as everyone from Hannibal Lecter to C.S. Lewis. 'Like a bomb waiting to explode,' says his frequent director Sir Richard Attenborough.

Clive Anderson | Sophie Balhetchet

Lawyer turned TV celeb – the most successful barrister on TV since John Mortimer – ('Whose Line Is It Anyway?' 'Clive Anderson Talks Back') who regards himself as 'a puppet on heat'. Brought up in Harrow by a Scots Presbyterian bank manager. Once asked Jeffrey Archer, 'Is there no beginning to your talent?' Currently making a BBC travel series.

Founder of Zed Limited with her partner Glenn Wilhide, pictured here, and acclaimed producer of 'The Camomile Lawn' and 'The Manageress'. One of her first roles on joining the industry was as coordinator of the Channel Four Group to establish an independent fourth channel, for which she then produced the first documentary commission and a run of films, series and features. Has since been Chairman of the Independent Programme Producers Association and course director at the National Film and Television School.

Richard Neat and David Moore

Met at Raymond Blanc's Le Manoir aux Quat' Saisons where Richard was *chef de partie* and David head waiter. In 1991 they took what might have seemed like a foolhardy step: to set up a restaurant – Pied-à-Terre – in London's West End in the midst of the worst recession most people can remember. They found a property in receivership, whitewashed the walls, hung a collection of modern art and opened the doors to serve creative modern French food that looks deceptively simple. It became a Michelin-starred restaurant within the first year. Thought by Jonathan Meades of *The Times* to 'deserve to become one of the London restaurants of the decade'.

Glenda Jackson

The most distinguished classical and modern actress of her generation, at least until she chose to disappear into the House of Commons at the last election, since when we have been waiting for her to take over her party's arts brief: we may now have to wait for the next election. Hampstead and Highgate's gain of a representative has been the theatre and cinema's loss of an actress who in everything from Peter Brook through Ken Russell to a touch of Hollywood class had established herself as Peggy Ashcroft's only real successor. Hopefully she'll eventually get back to where she belongs, on the other national stage.

Stewart Steven

Edited the *Mail on Sunday* for a decade, is now editor of the *Evening Standard*. A tough and crusading journalist at the respectable end of the tabloid market, he took understandable objection to Lord Marsh's recent assertion that 'a journalist's only duty is to provide the owners with an acceptable return on their investment'. Steven's *Standard* still fights for what is left of the best of London.

Peter Middleton

Chief Executive of Lloyd's during the worst period of its three-century life. Had to announce losses for 1991 of £2 billion. A maverick former monk with a penchant for motorbikes, he was an Olympic-class runner. Chose ten thousand cigarettes as his Desert Island luxury. Reckons Lloyd's will survive.

Sir Ron Dearing

Chairman of Camelot, the consortium which now runs the National Lottery. Before that, he ran the Post Office and sorted out John Patten's National Curriculum. A lifelong Methodist, he has never voted in a General Election for fear of then meeting someone he'd voted against. *The Times* reckons him pious, sober and industrious; unlikely therefore to scream 'Bingo' when they announce the winners.

Amanda Roocroft

Winner of the Kathleen Ferrier memorial prize and the Royal Philharmonic Award for her opera debut in 1990.
Since then she has been leading soprano for John Eliot Gardiner and Simon Rattle, and was in the Trevor Nunn
Cosi fan Tutte at Glyndebourne. Is barely thirty.

Greg Dyke | Leslie Waddington

Took nearly £10 million in shares when he left his post as Chief Executive at London Weekend in 1994 after the Granada takeover. Born in Hayes, Middlesex, he started out as a Marks & Spencer trainee, was on the dole at thirty, but then made his name with Roland, the only Rat ever to join a sinking ship, at TV-am. Then LWT, and the rest is takeover history.

Doyen of the London modern-art market, owner of the gallery he founded with his father, a figure of infinite knowledge and discretion. Born in Dublin in 1934, plays chess and backgammon. Don't ask, 'Is it a fake?'

Sir Walter Bodmer

Director General of the Imperial Cancer
Research Fund and a fan of *Jurassic Park*, even if
his DNA research suggests it may be a little
implausible. Has been studying DNA as the blue-
print for life since 1968 at Stanford. Wants above
all to make science more generally accessible. 'My
family seems to have no trouble, but then they are
nearly all geneticists or immunologists.'

Professor Sir Richard Doll

Now eighty-two, he was the first doctor
to establish the link between smoking and lung
cancer forty-three years ago. Son of a GP, he
carried morphine by hand to those on the retreat
from Dunkirk, and after the war took medical
research out of the laboratory and into society.
Approves of moderate drinking and crusades only
to make sure people know the risks of smoking.
'After that it's up to them.'

Terry Farrell

Architect of the new Charing Cross station and MI6 headquarters, he is one of Britain's most visible post-modernists. He is also building a £35 million Chester Arts Centre, one of the first bids for National Lottery funding, plus a new consulate in Hong Kong designed to affirm a continuing British presence to the incoming Chinese, albeit more economically than before.

Professor Michael Adler

Professor of Genito Urinary Medicine and Consultant Physician at the Middlesex since 1979. Educated at Bryanston, was a lecturer at St Thomas's, did pioneering Aids studies from 1985, served on the Terrence Higgins Trust and the Parliamentary all-party committee on Aids. Twice married, two daughters, likes Yoga and jogging.

Geoffrey Parsons

Australian pianist who has achieved cult status as one of the world's leading accompanists. Started with 'popular songs at a white piano under a chandelier' for £40 a week; progressed from there to Ann Ziegler and Webster Booth, then a residency with Elizabeth Schwarzkopf, and is now the most in-demand of all accompanists.

Raymond Gubbay

Concert promoter of considerable flair who has always taken a Classic FM view of life, even before they invented the radio station. Believes in music for all, not just 'South Bank snobs'. Takes a dim view of obscure Polish composers, reckoning it might be cheaper to send their likely British audience to Poland than bring the works here. Greatly enlivens the Barbican and Blenheim with massed bands of the Philharmonia and Robert Hardy as Churchill for ceremonial anniversaries.

Clive Gillinson

Former player with and now Managing Director of the London Symphony Orchestra, he is widely credited with turning their fortunes around and assuring their residency at the Barbican as well as on lucrative foreign tours and recording contracts. Ensures that high-profile conductors like André Previn and Michael Tilson Thomas are always around.

Nicholas Snowman

Chief Executive of the South Bank Centre. Before that, he created the London Sinfonietta and ran the Pierre Boulez music centre in Paris 1972-86. Distant cousin of Claire Bloom. Likes spy novels. Eager to make the South Bank more user-friendly, he has plans for pavement cafés, more walkways, less concrete and more carparks. Better weather might also help.

Paul Smith

Fashion designer credited with two main contributions to the twentieth century: spotted boxer shorts and primrose jumpers for men. Wanted to be a professional cyclist, but turned to fashion after a nasty crash left him in traction for seven months. Now he is the king of retail menswear with an annual turnover of £54 million on a business he started in 1970 with £600.

Richard Eyre and Genista McIntosh

Third director of the National Theatre after Olivier and Hall, and in many ways the most successful, if only because he has been able to learn from their mistakes: less inclined to be confrontational, doesn't disappear too often to Glyndebourne or Hollywood, maintains a strong balance of commerce and courage on all three stages. His current predilection is for American drama, everything from *Angels in America* to *Sweet Bird of Youth* and the latest Miller crossing. Reckons he'll return to the freelance life 'in another three years or so'. Describes himself as a liberal anarchist, but has given the NT more stability and success than at any time in its thirty-year span. Thanks also to his administrator Genista McIntosh, ex-RSC, seen with him here.

Sir Andrew Hugh-Smith

Chairman of the London Stock Exchange 1988-94, before that instrumental at
Courtaulds in bringing the WonderBra to Britain. Has no plans for retirement.
'It would be like running into a brick wall at sixty miles an hour.'

Lord Alexander of Weedon

Chairman of the NatWest, created a life peer in 1988, this urbane barrister was brought
in to restore the bank's somewhat shaken image. Personal details of height, three marriages and tennis
game are not, he tells journalists, what he cares to reveal. Other interests include Justice, the all-party
legal reform group, last resort of the aggrieved. A future Lord Chancellor?

Chryssie Fitzgerald | Stephen Twigg

Is on reflection a reflexologist, deeply into 'self-empowerment of the individual'. Born in Wales, has been involved in alternative medicine for ten years. Uses herbal remedies and believes in self-maintenance rather than doctors.

A wholly holistic massage and health consultant who offers 'body structure therapy with diet advice and mind- management training to bring about far-reaching health improvement and personal management'. Probably not your man for a five-course lunch at the Garrick with cigars and brandy. Hopes to retreat from London and teach in a 'more life-enhancing place'.

Sir Norman Foster

The richest and most desired architect in the world. Son of a Manchester factory worker, he spent
a lonely childhood reading about Frank Lloyd Wright. Studied at Yale with Richard Rogers. Recently won
the contract to redesign the British Museum Reading Room. Flies his bicycle to Switzerland for holidays.
His best-known buildings are Stanstead Airport and the Sainsbury Visual Arts Centre in Norwich.

Trevor McDonald

Sole anchor of 'News at Ten' since 1992, he is fifty-three, married with one son, and the celebrated interviewer of Nelson Mandela and Saddam Hussein. Brought up in Trinidad, where he started as a radio disc-jockey; he now lives in Surrey, has an OBE, and has written cricketing biographies of Viv Richards and Clive Lloyd. Was once offered a job by Gaddafi; turned it down.

Sarah Hogg | Steve Jones

Head of John Major's Policy Unit until 1994, and widely known as his Madame Svengali, the unofficial deputy PM. A former journalist (*Times*, *Independent*, *Economist*, Channel 4), she led an inner cabinet of politicians and civil servants. Father is Lord Boyd-Carpenter, father-in-law Lord Hailsham, husband Minister of State at the Foreign Office: what the Americans call well-connected.

Author of *The Language of the Genes*, which sets out to prove that the mysteries of mankind are to be solved not by archaeology but by genetics. 1991 Reith Lecturer. Special-study subjects include fruit flies, snails and slugs.

Sir Anthony Caro

The elder statesman of British sculpture, this is the man who kicked away the plinth and made the case for full abstraction. Now seventy, he read engineering at Cambridge and studied under Henry Moore. In the 1960s, his brightly painted welded-steel constructions changed the face of sculpture. He is now working on the Trojan War: thirty-eight figures from Homer's *Iliad* in steel, clay and wood.

Nicholas Serota

Director of the Tate Gallery, impresario of the Turner Prize, infinitely committed to the shock of the new,
but studied Turner at the Courtauld. In his six years at the Tate, he has regularly been under siege from critics:
'If I'm not being criticized, then I'm not doing my job properly.' Has been offered the New York Museum of Modern
Art, but wants to open one here first, either next to the Hayward Gallery or across from St Paul's.

WITHDRAWN

FASHION

AUSTRALIAN & NEW ZEALAND DESIGNERS

MITCHELL OAKLEY SMITH

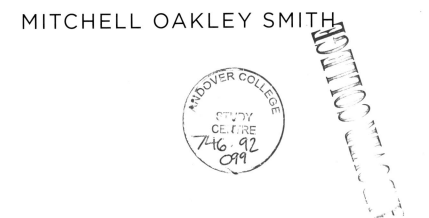
❧ Thames & Hudson

First published in Australia in 2010
by Thames & Hudson Australia Pty Ltd
11 Central Boulevard Portside Business Park
Fishermans Bend Victoria 3207
ABN: 72 004 751 964

www.thameshudson.com.au

Editing: Melinda Crimp
Design: Allyson Crimp
Production: Imago Australia Pty Ltd
Printed and bound in Singapore

ISBN: 9 7805 0050 0248

National Library of Australia Cataloguing-in-Publication entry

Oakley Smith, Mitchell.
FASHION : Australian and New Zealand designers / Mitchell Oakley Smith.
9 7805 0050 0248 (pbk.)
Fashion designers--Australia.
Fashion designers--New Zealand.
Fashion.
Fashion--Australia.
Fashion--New Zealand.
746.92

FASHION

Thames & Hudson

CONTENTS

This book is dedicated to all of the creative people who continue to inspire and allow us to dream.

NOTES

Australian Fashion Week refers to Rosemount Australian Fashion Week, Sydney, which was previously known as Mercedes Australian Fashion Week

Melbourne Fashion Festival refers to L'Oreal Melbourne Fashion Festival

TAFE Design Institute was previously known as East Sydney TAFE

RMIT University was previously known as Royal Melbourne Institute of Technology

New Zealand Fashion Week refers to Air New Zealand Fashion Week, Auckland

Seasons referenced throughout the book are as per the southern hemisphere unless specified.

INTRODUCTION

The work of local fashion designers has a unique identity and place in the international market. In many countries, fashion is an ingrained part of cultural identity, tied up in a sweeping national aesthetic and steeped in history. Australian and New Zealand fashion designers offer a much broader interpretation of our own identity. Drawing upon a mix of race, culture, gender and religion, these designers have created something particularly unique across many varied genres and styles.

When I first began writing this book, nearly everyone questioned my motivations. 'Are there *really* enough fashion designers in Australia and New Zealand to fill a book?' they enquired sceptically. It seems proof enough that the large extent of this book hasn't compromised the richly varied, talented and deserving designers within it. Although of a high international standard and with a large – and continually growing – export market, it seems there remains a cultural cringe when it comes to antipodean fashion. This is particularly highlighted by our penchant for big-name international brands as opposed to niche, local labels.

And yet fashion in the region is growing at an exceptional rate. In just a decade, Australian Fashion Week, which opened to negative criticism in 1996, has grown into a thriving, week-long celebration of the designers showcased. Similarly, New Zealand Fashion Week plays a pivotal role in promoting its designers. Both events continually attract buyers and reporters from the world's biggest sales and media outlets that relay the excitement of the events to the general public. While the success of fashion in these countries cannot be entirely attributed to such events, it is mutually acknowledged that Australian

1 Silk dress and Egyptian cotton leggings
with print by Del Kathryn Barton,
Romance Was Born, S/S 05/06

2 Silk organza, silk tulle, silk gauze, wool and printed lace gown, J'Aton Couture, A/W 07

and New Zealand Fashion Weeks act as a catalyst of inspiration and confidence for the broader industry.

Professor Roy Greene's 2008 *Review of Australia's Textile, Clothing and Footwear Industries* (TCF) found that TCF output in Australia is valued at $2.8 billion, with retail and wholesale sectors adding another $7.5 billion. What's more is that these industries employ over 200 000 people. Creativity aside, such information speaks of the growing success of our fashion industry. Beyond this, the number of enrolments at fashion schools continues to grow year upon year, not only in design but the connected creative industries of styling, make-up artistry and photography. Such increased popularity is mirrored in public fashion and retail events.

More than this, fashion reaches beyond just clothing. Cultural shifts in the past decade have seen fashion considered and respected as a valid art form, in several cases entering the artistic sphere through gallery-style exhibition and appraisal. A 2009 exhibition at the National Gallery of Victoria, *Together Alone*, showcased eight prominent designers from Australia and New Zealand, including Romance Was Born, Toni Maticevski and Zambesi. In the same year, a retrospective of Easton Pearson collections was shown at Brisbane's Gallery of Modern Art, celebrating the brand's trademark weaving of Asian Pacific cultures through its collections. It was the clothes themselves that garnered the attention of visitors and media alike: here, Easton Pearson's signature styles and ideas remained strongly central to the development of their collections, each interpreted and executed in fresh and relevant ways. In mainstream media, too, fashion is more popular than ever before, particularly with involvement of audiences in television programs such as *Project Runway* and *Australia's Next Top Model.* The breakdown of the barrier that once existed between the secular fashion industry and the general public has been seen as the democratisation of fashion. Not detrimental to its growth or prestige, local fashion has gained the attention, interest and, ultimately, respect of its public.

On an international level there is great interest in Australian and New Zealand fashion designers. There is something very special about an industry when many of its leading labels – such as Aurelio Costarella, Josh Goot, Willow and Toni Maticevski – are showing on international runways to great acclaim. Beyond this, Australian fashion icon Collette Dinnigan serves as a member of the Chambre Syndicale in Paris, the governing body of the French fashion industry. The great contribution of such designers to the fashion world is welcomed, applauded and, by now, expected – for nowhere else in the world is there a climate or landscape like that of Australia. Nor is there such a close and complementing combination of European and Eastern cultures and influences, uniquely combined with our own Indigenous heritage. From a style viewpoint, the unique trends produced are reflective of the cultural mish-mash of the region.

Before this book, there had not been a singular resource for fashion design in Australia and New

3 Silk and chiffon dress,
Marnie Skillings, S/S 08/09

4 Rib pleated shift dress in silk gazar,
Dion Lee, A/W 10

Zealand for nearly three decades. Despite the excellent quality of local magazines – and indeed, Australia and New Zealand are the highest consumers of magazines in the world – this type of publication fails to categorically and wholly represent such a broad industry. In saying that, this book does not, and never did, intend to cover each and every designer in the local market, for such a task would be nigh impossible. Instead, this book aims to provide a clear and relevant cross-section of contemporary fashion design in the region. *FASHION* provides, beyond our own wardrobes, a tangible reference for students, retailers, consumers and fellow creatives to look to for information and inspiration. It is dedicated to and inspired by the designers it profiles; evidence of the ever-increasing value (both creative and commercial) of an industry that has flourished in a region that has not traditionally embraced its own artistic talents. As a collective promotion of our image makers, this book is long overdue.

Profiled are designers across a broad range of styles – womenswear, menswear, eveningwear, swimwear, haute couture and streetwear. It follows those producing their first commercial collections, as well as those who have weathered over 30 years in the industry. Each and every one of the 70 designers featured in *FASHION* reveals that their influences are unlike any other in the world, and therefore, so is their clothing. From the timeless classicism of J'Aton Couture's glamour and Aurelio Costarella's contrasting of decadent and elegant tailoring, through to a newer generation of artists – the kitsch eccentricity of Romance Was Born and the highly structured modernity of Dion Lee – these artists capture the zeitgeist by reinterpreting standard wardrobe staples in innovative and clever ways, season upon season.

The purpose of this book is to break down the perceptions of local fashion and communicate its unique voice; to bring you face-to-face with the incredibly talented artists that have not only created wearable collections, but also allowed us to dream, to be inspired and to learn to appreciate. All the while these designers have unearthed the international myths of the Australian region and its people, modestly promoting a forward-thinking, cosmopolitan nation. These designers are real, and their creativity unlimited. They work in their own shops, they cut and sew, they answer the phones, and, as I'm proud to note, they do it with a sense of humour.

5 Silk dress, Josh Goot, A/W 08

6 Silk dress, Josh Goot, A/W 08

AKIRA
AKIRA ISOGAWA

One of Australia's most famed designers, Akira Isogawa's work defines a stylistic genre of clothing representative of cultural marriage. Of Japanese heritage, Isogawa immigrated to Australia in 1986, where he studied fashion design at the TAFE Design Institute. In 1993, the young designer opened his first boutique in Sydney's Woollahra, launching the label that soon came to be known simply as Akira.

As the designer reflects, 'I started my own label really low key, without much expectation. I didn't even have time to think about what may happen with my work.' Indeed, Isogawa was responsible for creating and producing his own collections, as well as working in his boutique. Isogawa's designs gained a strong following in the initial years after launching, positioning him centrally in the great progression of Australian fashion in the mid-1990s. Since then, Isogawa's design and business have continued to flourish, now represented in high-end boutiques throughout the world and with four stand-alone stores in Australia. Isogawa believes the change he has witnessed in the industry over the course of his career is that 'it is not as naïve as it was. When I have a look around the cities in Australia, the choices are much more vast. It's become more savvy.'

Isogawa describes his work as 'timeless,' noting that he frequently receives comments from customers that they wear pieces from various collections many years after purchase. 'They bring it back another year,' he explains, 'maybe not frequently, because the designs are quite specific, but in that way they are timeless and quite individual.' The concept of timelessness seems inherently relevant to Isogawa's clothes, given their unique nature not only in terms of thematic or stylistic expression, but in the complex

1 Silk chiffon
dress with
embroidered
waist, A/W 09

2 Printed two-layer kimono
coat, silk jacquard dress and
vintage obi belt, S/S 09/10

level of construction, use of textiles and hand-detailing. With a base of predominantly natural materials such as silk, wool, cotton and linen – with the addition of 'certain man-made fibres like Lycra or nylon for practicality and stretch' – Isogawa makes use of hand-manipulation to 'create the desirable shape' of each garment. Such techniques include origami-inspired folding ('a paper technique that I translate in textiles') and smocking, as well as embellishment with hand-embroidery using beads and glass.

Isogawa finds inspiration in travelling and, more specifically, the people, techniques and practices he discovers along the way: 'perhaps visiting the people who produce hand-crafted textiles, which could be in India or Japan,' he offers. 'It could be anywhere in the world. I just find rare textiles,

hand-crafted by people, and that experience of working with them quite inspirational.' This, combined with the designer's Japanese heritage, is perhaps what differentiates his work so distinctly from the surrounding fashion climate. Drawing upon traditional costume from his native Japan, the designer creates garments that simultaneously respond to the relaxed Australian aesthetic and that can be introduced into wardrobes of women and men the world over.

This is not to say that Isogawa's work is disqualified from heralding or responding to trends. Rather, the simplicity and beauty of his clothes is an overriding quality. 'When I design clothes, I don't necessarily take trend into consideration so heavily,' explains Isogawa. 'I think it's good to be aware of what's going on, and it's great to wear fashion sometimes for the sake of a moment, because it can be fun! But my approach toward design is a particular attitude. As much as I love seeing a customer appreciating what I do, at the end of the day I need to be fully satisfied with my own design. I call my work an expression of who I am or where I am at.'

Isogawa shows his collections twice yearly in Paris, where he has a showroom for international buyers and has established an international reputation for himself and his work. 'When I first showed in Paris in the late 1990s, there was a bit of confusion. It was really hard work, especially not knowing what was going on with the language barrier.' Today, Isogawa works with a regular team and finds the exercise of showing his collections abroad an enjoyable experience, particularly for the travel. The Akira label has also shown at Australian Fashion Week since its inception in 1996.

For his dedication and contribution to Australian fashion, Isogawa has been honoured with several exhibitions dedicated to his work by galleries including the National Gallery of Victoria (NGV), the Powerhouse Museum, Sydney, and Object Gallery, Sydney. 'To be approached by the arts sector,' Isogawa tells, 'and for the opportunity to prove my work in a rare or unique environment [other than] fashion, I am flattered.' The 2004-2005 *Printemps-Eté* exhibition at the NGV was the first solo fashion and textiles exhibition by an Australian designer at a major national or state institution. The gravity of such an event is testament to the importance and lasting nature of Isogawa's work. Given such exposure in both the fashion and arts sectors, it stands to reason that the designer was honoured by Australia Post, with Isogawa's image appearing on a commemorative Australian Legend postage stamp in 2005. In 2007, the designer was granted the Australian Fashion Laureate for his contribution to the Australian fashion industry. For the future, however, the designer insists that he is 'not the sort of person that has a big plan. I just wish that in years to come – 20 years' time, even – I'm still inspired to design brilliant work, to design great collections. And to be appreciated by not only Australia but in beautiful cities around the world.'

'AS MUCH AS I LOVE SEEING A
CUSTOMER APPRECIATING WHAT
I DO, AT THE END OF THE DAY
I NEED TO BE FULLY SATISFIED
WITH MY OWN DESIGN'
– *Akira Isogawa*

3 Cotton jacket and embroidered
cotton cropped pants,
S/S 07 (northern hemisphere)

ALICE McCALL

ALICE McCALL

A chance job as a stylist in London unfolded a series of events that would lead Alice McCall to launch her own fashion label in 2004. What distinguishes McCall from many designers is her natural ability to represent the epoch by combining stylistic elements in such a way that appeals to a great audience.

As McCall explains, 'design is in my blood. I grew up on a Singer sewing machine, and both my mum and my sister are fashion designers.' A younger McCall spent a year studying art foundation at Wimbledon College in London before landing the styling job with MTV London. Here, McCall was responsible for dressing the presenters on the hip music program. Over the next decade, McCall continued her career as a stylist, working with the likes of *Dazed and Confused* magazine, musicians Destiny's Child and Blondie, and advertising campaigns for Levi's, Nike and Rimmel. It was during this successful tenure as a stylist that McCall began making one-off silk tops and 1950s-style customised dresses. These pieces caught the attention of many in McCall's immediate clique, later selling through London boutiques Pinneal Eye and Euphoria.

Having made a name for herself in the United Kingdom, McCall was headhunted to design the Spring/Summer 2002/2003 collection for popular label Buddhist Punk. This collection, which demonstrated McCall's dual design and styling ability, gained international recognition and demand. McCall was headhunted yet again the following year, designing two collections for Australian label sass & bide. In 2004, McCall launched her own label at Australian Fashion Week. As McCall recounts of the first show, 'it was a great springboard, and directly after we sold to

'LONGEVITY AND SUSTAINABILITY ARE THE TRUE TEST'
– Alice McCall

1 Party 08

department stores David Jones, Barneys New York and Harrods London.' And while McCall has shown her collection in London since her 2004 launch, she strongly supports Australian Fashion Week and intends to continue showing at the event in the future. Such presentations demand the best of a designer, inspiring them to grow and develop. 'I think fashion is somewhat fickle, and so longevity and sustainability are the true test,' she says. McCall's business today has maintained its momentum. The designer says her developments have been 'with equal focus on the inward - the business foundation, range planning, production and margins – as with the outward: design, public relations, brand signature. These are the key things in the development and sustainability of the label.'

The success of the Alice McCall label, believes its designer, is the 'perfect balance of signature and reinvention.' And yet the clothes, while appreciated for their unique take on trends and offbeat personality, are essentially basic wardrobe garments. 'I think about what I want to wear, what is missing from my wardrobe,' says McCall, noting that one-off craft pieces found at flea markets inspire the individuality inherent in her designs. A unique blend of bohemian, rock and roll and feminine elements, the charm of Alice McCall is in the details: of laser cut-outs and embroidery, one-off artist-designed prints and unexpected zips. 'Krowang is a cutwork technique that we have become quite well known for,' explains McCall, 'as well as different knitting techniques, beading and appliqués.' And as quirky as the design influences is Alice McCall's customer base: 'from teens to forties.'

3 A/W 10

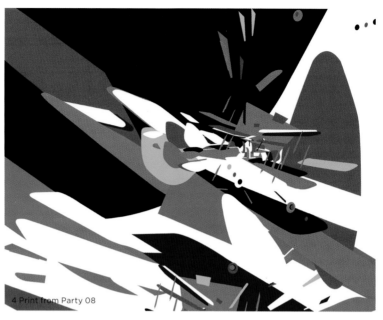

4 Print from Party 08

5 A/W 10

6 A/W 0[...]

7 Party 08

ALPHA60
ALEX AND GEORGIE CLEARY

Evolving from graphic-printed t-shirts, siblings Alex and Georgie Cleary's Alpha60 has become one of Australia's most popular labels, known for its high quality offering of wardrobe standards in an unwavering colour palette of black and white. Strongly influenced by iconic films, the Alpha60 world is in itself cinematic, employing highly visual elements in each collection.

Whilst the first t-shirts under the name Alpha60 were made in 2001, it wasn't until 2004 that the hobby became a business for Alex and Georgie. This initial entry into the market, on the cusp of the hugely popular trend of printed tees, was a case of excellent timing. And while graphics remain a largely central part of the Alpha60 aesthetic, the collections – both men's and women's – are more structured. 'We have learnt as we went along,' explains Alex. 'What we've developed is a lot more formal in terms of design because it has matured with us from just prints on tees.' The formality that Alex refers to isn't in the sense of attire – the few suits that exist within the collection are more deconstructed than they are formal – but of the way in which they present their work each season. While new ideas and styles are played upon, there remains a consistent dialogue between the men's and women's collections and with collections past, continually building upon Alpha60's recognisable aesthetic. 'It's not typically androgynous,' says Alex. 'Not downing the brands that do that, it's great, but it's not our style; we essentially design for ourselves and what we want to wear.' It makes sense, then, that the designers claim that their work is not driven by fashion itself, but inspired by art, music and movies. 'We can't and don't pick a style or reference and run with that. That doesn't work. Instead we splice lots of ideas and subtle influences.' Such influences include, for the Spring/Summer 2009/2010 season, renowned French film director Jean-Luc Godard.

1 Silk jacket, silk top
and cotton skirt,
A/W 07

The basis of the Alpha60 collection of
casual separates and accessories has
remained constant since its inception
in a palette of black, white and
occasionally grey, which they believe
is a strong part of their identity and
reflects their Melbourne base.
They believe, too, that this need not
be changed, noting that New Zealand
brands Zambesi and NOM*d remain
cutting-edge after 20 years and have
never strayed from their singular
vision, a central reason for their
success. 'That's really where we'd like
to be,' the Clearys add. The designers
don't feel defined by their being
Australian, and have found on a world
stage that they do in fact compare
well to other brands by remaining
true to themselves.

While the collection has subtly
and gently matured, so too has
its customer base, still strongly
consisting of 20-30 year olds that
are interested in fashion, but right

2 Silk dress
with digital print,
S/S 09/10

'WE ESSENTIALLY
DESIGN FOR
OURSELVES AND
WHAT WE WANT
TO WEAR...
WE SPLICE A
LOT OF IDEAS
AND SUBTLE
INFLUENCES'
– *Alex Cleary*

3 Silk jersey
dress, S/S 09/10

through to people in their sixties, according to the designers. 'We don't cater to any particular market, and that's because there are two of us designing.' Alpha60's audience has broadened with the assistance of retailers General Pants Co. and Sportsgirl, with whom the designers have collaborated. For General Pants Co., Alpha60 produce a diffusion line of their brand called the beta state, which shares a similar aesthetic to Alpha60 but caters to a younger audience in its choice of fabrics and styles and, subsequently, lower price points. As a one-off capsule collection in early 2010, Alpha60 worked with Sportsgirl. According to Alex, 'there is no dilution of the brand' with such collaborations, but rather, they 'give the brand great exposure. People that aren't in

cities and haven't heard of Alpha60 might gain a little confidence in the brand by buying an Alpha60 for Sportsgirl t-shirt, and so one day if they walk past our own boutique, they might have the confidence and interest to come in. We want to make it accessible to people.'

Retail is an area in which Alpha60 stand out in the Australian market, and in early 2010 opened their sixth domestic store and were also nominated for Ragtrader's Retailer of the Year award. The Alpha60 stores, aptly titled Alphaville, are designed by Alex and Georgie with the intention of making them conceptually interesting, yet welcoming to the customer. And although they would 'love to open shops in New York and London,' they are currently focused on developing their presence and

4 Graphic from Alpha60 for Sportsgirl collection, 2010

5 (From left) Cotton jersey singlet, scarf and pants; cotton jersey dress, S/S 06/07

customer base on a domestic level. In doing this, and working alongside the likes of General Pants Co., they have been able to learn and perfect their methods of production and delivery, earning them international stockists in the likes of Liberty of London. 'They don't usually go for unknown brands, and watch you for a few seasons before they invest. We're not funded by anyone, so we've had to grow slowly and do things ourselves. What we really want is a solid base here in Australia and then to gradually grow internationally.'

While Alex and Georgie have never defined their roles within the business ('which breaks every rule of partnership'), Georgie essentially manages the design aspect of the clothing, while Alex works more on the business, branding, retail stores and shows. 'We've got exactly the same goals, and we respect each other so much and always help each other with what we're doing. It's so busy, but what we do just meshes nicely. We both wish we had the chance to design more!' Yet clothes make up only a part of the Alpha60 brand, with other areas, such as the interactive website, retail stores and fashion shows, which create the brand narrative. 'It's part of the feel and is really exciting,' says Alex.

ANNA & BOY
LILL BOYD AND ANNA HEWETT

Frustrated by the lack of style-conscious swimwear available in Australia, Lill Boyd and Anna Hewett, then colleagues at *Vogue* Australia, left their day jobs to create a label that addressed this gap in the swimwear market. Launching their first small collection in late 2005, Anna & Boy seamlessly combines fashion concepts with swimwear in innovative, brilliant prints of the highest quality Italian and French fabrics with unique detailing.

It seems a clever career change to move from fashion editorial to fashion design, for not only do Boyd and Hewett have a vested interest in the industry, but an understanding of what works stylistically and (just as importantly) commercially. Working together for two years, the duo created the still-life market pages of *Vogue* Australia which included a seasonal swim round-up. 'We would compile the pages and shoots and that's where the frustration grew from,' recounts Hewett. 'There were only a few fashion/swimwear brands in the market, and there wasn't anything tailored to what we, or our friends, would like to wear. Our boyfriends, too, had no options when it came to shorts outside of 'surf' brands. That's where Anna & Boy came from.'

Interested in fashion and design whilst growing up, neither Boyd or Hewett had ever considered a career in design specifically, but had both wanted to be in the surrounding creative industries. It was their desire to create something for themselves, and for those in a similar position, that led to the creation of their swim label. 'We knew how to tailor the brand in a way that appealed to our ex-colleagues and those in media,' which proved to be of great help to the fledgling business. 'We put together a tiny collection with no idea of what we were doing.' Fortunately for the

1 Polyester and
Lycra bikini, S/S 09/10

2 Polyester swim
shorts, S/S 09/10

3 Cotton and Lycra
bikini, S/S 06/07

designers, Anna & Boy was bought
by several stores throughout
Australia within its first season,
leading them to show at Australian
Fashion Week in 2006 with a
spectacular presentation staged
at the Sydney Opera House. 'It
was our launching pad and was
a great forum to show everyone
what we were doing.' The pair has
since continued to show as part of
Australian Fashion Week, reaching
national fashion press and appealing
to their international clients.

As they build their business, the
designers have been careful about
where their brand sits, wanting for
their product to be accessible, but
not targeted to mass consumption.

'The growth has been quite slow,
it's pretty organic. We're holding
back till we're ready because we're
learning as we go.' says Hewett.
This style of business seems
tailored to the duo's approach to
design, which is fashionable but not
slavishly driven by trend. 'There is
only so much change in swimwear
each season before you confuse
your customers,' tells Hewett. 'They
[customers] want to find the shapes
they liked the season before, and
so the prints we design are the
seasonal focus. It comes from a
strong idea: themes accumulate
and come together to create a feel
or mood that both Lill and I share.'

Whilst swimwear uses minimal
pieces of fabric, the designers
don't feel limited in their creative
vision. Prints allow Boyd and
Hewett to express their ideas
each season, which, while always
different, are strongly influenced
by memories of childhood, such as

4 Polyester and Lycra
one-piece swimsuit, Cruise 10

'beach house wallpapers, seventies surf films and yellowed photographs that wistfully capture that time,' they explain, referring to the period of social change that promoted freedom and youth. Such ideals are perfectly suited to the beach culture they foster through the creation of swimwear. Created in high-quality fabrics with special finishes – clever swing tags, zip-lock travel bags and gold peach trinkets – Anna & Boy has created a unique signature that underlies their design philosophy.

In addition to swimwear, Anna & Boy also offer clothing components and a winter collection, comparable to a European cruise collection, consisting of outerwear in heavier fabrics. For the future, the duo plan to grow the fashion aspect of their business, adding more clothes that correlate with the main swim lines. 'For us, we have the headspace of an urban beach girl, which includes fashion. We want to develop the clothing aspect of the business, as well as the prints and swimwear, to create a bigger lifestyle collection – strengthening the brand and explaining it more with clothing.'

5 Polyester and Lycra one-piece swimsuit, S/S 09/10

'THE BEACH IS SO INTERTWINED WITH OUR DAILY LIFE THAT IT MAKES SENSE FOR US TO HAVE FASHION SWIMWEAR' – *Anna Hewett*

ANT!PODiUM
GEOFFREY J. FINCH

Despite its relative youth in the marketplace, Geoffrey J. Finch's label ANT!PODiUM has gained a considerable following around the world, due largely to the confidence of the designs and the unique nature of the business. Such confidence comes not from extensive study or support, for Finch did not study fashion, but rather an understanding of the label's place in the market, upon which Finch builds strongly.

Conceived in 2006 between Shoreditch, East London and Fremantle, Western Australia, the womenswear label ANT!PODiUM is the worldly love child of an unconventional design relationship between Australian expats Geoffrey J. Finch and sisters Ashe Peacock, and Fremantle-based Fenella Peacock. The collective was originally established in 2003 as a London-based retail store, and PR and wholesale agency for Australian and New Zealand fashion. The independent clothing line began not as a vanity project but to 'fill the racks between the existing collections,' explains Finch. Fenella, who was behind the successful 1980s label Empire Line, created the first capsule offering based on Finch's drawings, and a label was born. The success is particularly remarkable and perhaps due to the fact that Finch is not formally trained, 'apart from a few sewing and drawing classes while on exchange in France.' The son of a dressmaker, Finch grew up surrounded by fabrics, patterns, sewing machines and 'those really large format issues of *Mode* magazine.'

Finch's isolated upbringing in rural Queensland, combined with his international travels and collaborative work style, has resulted in a unique aesthetic that is 'very much a combination of a London sensibility and nonchalant Australian chic.' Inspired by the group of artists and

1 Print from A/W 09

2 Opening of S/S 09/10
collection presentation at
Australian Fashion Week

creatives that have formed around ANT!PODiUM, the style of the clothing reflects the nature of the business, with pieces simultaneously confident and humorous. This compellingly modern and unaffected approach to fashion has seen the label garner great success for its distinct wearability and accessibility. The collections are somewhat androgynous, but not in the sense of deconstructed, black clothing. Instead, Finch's designs adopt traditional menswear – and, to some extent, boy's clothing – and interpret this in more feminine, sexy ways: ripped denim shorts, sheer, oversized t-shirts, track-shape pants with elastic-banded ankles in sheer fabrics with knee patches. Through this approach Finch exposes and conceals the female form to reveal, sometimes only fleetingly, her most flattering shapes and proportions. Based between two countries,

ANT!PODiUM has been able to approach several markets at once, gaining stockists in the likes of Harvey Nichols, Liberty of London, Lane Crawford and David Jones after only two years. As Finch tells, 'the experience gained from working overseas has allowed us to expand at the rate we have.' When the first styles made it in-store, British *Vogue* were the first to catch on, encouraging the trio to officially launch their label at London Fashion Week of the same year, which they did to overwhelming acclaim. 'We thought we really might be onto something at this stage,' adds Finch of the rapid initial growth. Through Australian Fashion Week ANT!PODiUM has

3 Cotton pants
and cropped
cotton jacket,
S/S 10 (northern
hemisphere)

raised a strong profile in the local market, finding support in QANTAS, in winning the 2008 Spirit of Youth Award (SOYA), which includes a cash prize, international flights and industry mentorship for a year. 'It was a total honour to win. Many people love our passion and unique approach, and the wise advice from older hands is extraordinarily invaluable.' ANT!PODiUM was also nominated for the prestigious 2009 Designer Award, presented by Woolmark and supported by *Vogue* Australia at the Melbourne Fashion Festival.

Described by *i-D* magazine as 'entrepreneurs of the London fashion world,' the future looks exceptionally bright for the fashion collective. Future plans include more of the infamous No Romance parties, relaunching ANT!PODiUM magazine, and consolidating stockists in the UK and Australia whilst laying the foundations for commercial growth in the USA. Creativity, however, is still at the fore of all ventures.

'I CONSIDERED STUDYING LAW,
BUT REALISED IT WAS ONLY THE RAZZY
SUITS THAT I WAS ACTUALLY KEEN ON'
– *Geoffrey J. Finch*

4 Cotton skirt, cotton shirt
and wool jacket,
S/S 10 (northern hemisphere)

ARNSDORF
JADE SARITA ARNOTT

Arnsdorf's Jade Sarita Arnott is a designer of a rare nature, for she not only understands but also acknowledges the place, value and function of fashion in contemporary society. As she explains, 'I have a respect for the modern archetypal wardrobe garments – trench coats, tailored pants, blouses and the like; the costumes of our daily lives. I like creating something new every season, but am conscious that the pieces have to fit back into people's wardrobes. I have a respect for the wearer and how [the garment] will complement their life.' If fashion is the one design genre that must successfully marry commercial and functional value with artistic vision, Sarita Arnott's work is the best possible example of how to do so.

Launched in 2007 upon Sarita Arnott's graduation from fashion school, the name Arnsdorf is her family's original surname that was changed upon migration to Australia. Sarita Arnott studied extensively in the creative industries: first at the Victorian College of the Arts (VCA), majoring in creative writing, art and film, and later at RMIT University in fashion design. 'It was a lot of studying,' admits Sarita Arnott. 'But once I had decided that I wanted to go in the direction of fashion and of having my own label, I knew it was important to go and learn the skills.' Such a lengthy course of study may seem irrelevant to Sarita Arnott's product today, but in actuality, her success may well be attributed to her training, which not only allowed her the time and creative freedom to explore her artistic ideas, but also provided her with a broader understanding of the demands of the fashion market. Sarita Arnott's training gave her the confidence to launch a business and to create clothing that is of outstanding quality in its design and technicality.

It makes sense that Sarita Arnott would choose a creative field for her career path, given that her artist parents always encouraged and applauded creativity from a young age. 'I was always interested in art,' she explains. 'And I always had an interest in fashion, but it wasn't until later that I fully understood it and considered it as a career.' Even today, given Sarita Arnott's broad interests and influences, fashion remains only a portion of her creative energies. It's perhaps because of this that the Arnsdorf label is free of commercially-driven trends. In the relatively small Australian market, a point

'I HAVE A
RESPECT FOR
THE MODERN
ARCHETYPAL
WARDROBE
GARMENTS...
THE COSTUMES
OF OUR
DAILY LIVES'
– *Jade Sarita
Arnott*

2 Sheer silk shirt, denim
shorts and leather belt,
S/S 09/10

of difference from the many labels that follow international trends is greatly welcomed. Hence, there's been a positive reaction to Sarita Arnott's work from the very beginning. 'It's a lot of hard work, but I've been quite lucky from the start,' says the modest designer. 'Most people have been really supportive. When [high end Melbourne boutique] Marais picked me up in my first season, I knew I was on the right track, and just built from there.'

2009 marked the first on-schedule fashion show for Arnsdorf at Australian Fashion Week. This collection was Sarita Arnott's most realised and well-executed to date, cementing her position in the local industry and reaching international buyers and press. As Sarita Arnott

tells, putting together a collection and a show is 'very nerve-wracking. You don't have time to make things perfectly or how you first imagined. But it's a great opportunity, and a lot of people learnt about my work from that show.' The collection, titled *And You Love,* was inspired by the concept and pursuit of considered danger and moving forward. 'It's about taking a risk which may seem dangerous, but that is actually more dangerous or risky not to take. They are themes which seem to run through my own life and seem relevant.' Interestingly, the colours of the collection were the boldest to date, which seems reflective of the theme that Sarita

4 Linen shirt,
denim shorts and
leather belt, S/S 09/10

3 Cotton shirt,
denim jeans and
leather belt, A/W 09

Arnott is playing on. Sarita Arnott continues to explain that she was inspired by the form of ice-skating costumes and parachuters' equipment, drawing a link between the two as metaphors for 'pursuits that appeared risky, but on closer inspection would be more so if not undertaken with decisive precision and strength.' Like the explanation, the collection itself is precise, strong and a little risky, for it was a step away from her previous work. 'It was my intention to give the garments these qualities of elegance, fluidity, precision and strength, and empower the person wearing the clothes.' That Sarita Arnott is inspired by a feeling or idea, rather than something tangible, seems apt to the style of her clothing.

By using silk mesh, silk georgette and sand-washed silk, as well as organic linens, denim and thread lace, Sarita Arnott has referenced the sheer panels and cut-out shapes of ice-skating costumes and parachute strings, though it is executed in a way that is completely original. Adding to such originality is Sarita Arnott's use of colour. Everything in the Arnsdorf collection, past and present, has been custom-dyed based on the season's colour palette – evidence of Sarita Arnott's artistic eye and testament to her technical ability and dedication to quality. Throughout each season, Sarita Arnott uses organic fabrics such as linens, cotton silks and jerseys, and is drawn to a monochromatic colour palette that allows her to explore the complexities of tone, hue and saturation.

5 Jersey dress and wool blend jacket, A/W 09

Despite such particulars in the design process, Sarita Arnott admits that she doesn't have anyone specific in mind when she designs. 'The design is inspired by a feeling... I want it to be inclusive, sensititve, intelligent and strong. My intention is that I take them – my customers – on a journey each season, exploring an idea that feels close to me. I try to use the garments as a vehicle to explore themes and hopefully the customer can get a sense of that. It doesn't matter if people view it on a completely aesthetic level – the customer can decide what they want to appreciate and take away from it.'

That said, the clothes, on a purely aesthetic level, are simply beautiful, due in large part to the fabrics and colours used. Each piece retains a strong sense of classicism, modernised by a subtle subversion of the traditional form. 'I find function an important consideration, and it's about finding that balance of creating something new but that also fits into someone's life. For me, that's what makes fashion such an interesting medium to work in.'

6 Tencel-washed denim shirt and jeans, A/W 09

AURELIO COSTARELLA
RAY COSTARELLA

'I'm not looking to produce fashion that is trend-driven; my aim is to produce timeless pieces of clothing,' explains Ray Costarella, which suggests why his label, Aurelio Costarella, remains under the radar in Australia. Based in Perth to distance himself from the fashion scene, Costarella has produced exquisite women's clothing since 1984 and shows regularly as part of New York Fashion Week. He owns a traditional bespoke salon in Claremont, Perth, is successfully stocked throughout the USA, the Middle East and Italy, and is the only fashion designer listed on the Australian Stock Exchange.

Perhaps what is most interesting about Costarella's business is that he never thought about fashion in terms of a career, and yet more than two decades later he continues to create clothing that is decidedly different to what the Australian market typically prescribes or expects. Haute couture, with its intricate, exaggerated and heavily-structured detail, finds its roots in construction. It seems a relevant change of course for Costarella, who dropped out of architecture studies to dabble with a sewing machine, making clothes for friends and family and unknowingly teaching himself all that he knows today. In fact, the store he sold his first pieces to would later join in partnership with Costarella, who soon after bought the entire space.

The designer worked as a wholesaler throughout the early 1990s and opened two of his own stores to further establish his brand, one in Claremont and the other in Sydney's Strand Arcade. It was during this period of growth that the designer picked up several industry awards, including WA Designer of the Year (1995). When he found himself working as a business owner rather than a creative artist he decided to step back

1 Silk dress with metal beading, S/S 09/10

and complement the female form, rather than hang from it.

Costarella predominantly produces eveningwear as well as sophisticated daywear, though what makes his style so unique and highly regarded is the techniques and fabrics used. His manipulation of delicate bead work and authentic silks create beautiful gowns and coats reminiscent of a glamorous bygone era. Print is often kept to a minimum in the designer's work: 'it is more about the cut of a garment and those subtle details that really set it apart.' In a homecoming of sorts (for the designer regularly shows to high acclaim as part of New York Fashion Week) Costarella returned to Australian Fashion Week in 2009. 'Our focus had been promoting the label in the international arena,' he explains. '[But] with the changing economic climate in 2009, we thought it was important to support and strengthen our home base: local retailers and clients.' His regular clients wholeheartedly agree, with women from 16 to 60, and from all corners of the world, vying for his latest additions.

from retail to regroup. In 2000 Costarella launched his current label at Australian Fashion Week and, as the sole designer and creative visionary, it is a true representation of his style and talent.

Inspired by the light around him, Costarella begins working from a reference point. 'Be it a colour palette or a particular type of embroidery or beading, I find a beginning and work from there. Most often I work on the model, as I prefer to create in 3D rather than with a pattern. It's about playing with form.' Such a work style is reflected in his garments, which rely heavily on the draping, smocking and tucking of fabrics to accentuate

2 Silk dress, S/S 09/10

3 Silk dress with
embroidery and beaded
corset, S/S 09/10

4 Silk top and
embroidered and beaded
silk skirt, S/S 09/10

Costarella's 2009 Australian Fashion Week presentation allowed guests
to view and appreciate the exquisite pieces on statuesque models, and
gave us only a hint of what was to come in this season. Entitled *Morphosis*,
the summer collection was inspired by the work of Japanese architect
Tadao Ando, and demonstrated the evolution and growth of Costarella's
work as a designer. In a luscious colour palette of steel, bronze, copper,
honey and flame, each piece demonstrates Costarella's undeniable design
mastery, evidenced by high quality silks and natural fibres and made more
spectacular with the use of embroidery, beading and embellishment.
'Detail is paramount, but delicate in contrast to strong sculptural form,'
he explains.

5 Silk dress with metal beading, backstage at Australian Fashion Week, S/S 09/10

'MY WORK APPEALS TO WOMEN WHO APPRECIATE CLASSIC DESIGN WITH A POINT OF DIFFERENCE. EMBROIDERY, BEADING, SMOCKING AND CORSETRY COMBINED WITH EXQUISITE SILKS... IT IS OUR ATTENTION TO DETAIL THAT SETS US APART'
— *Ray Costarella*

6 S/S 09/10 collection presentation at Australian Fashion Week

7 Silk blouse with beaded corset and
linen and rayon skirt, S/S 09/10

BASSIKE
DEBORAH SAMS AND MARY LOU RYAN

Noting a considerable gap in the Australian market for high-quality wardrobe staples, Deborah Sams and Mary Lou Ryan paired together to create bassike. Offering simple men's and women's wear in cleverly designed silhouettes, bassike clothing is created entirely from organic cotton jersey. As a result, the product is not only luxurious in wear but represents an international movement in ecologically sustainable clothing production.

The bassike name derives from the concept of 'basics', upon which the brand is built. But while focused on particular pieces of clothing – tees, pants, sweaters, et al – each season presents a new dimension in the constantly evolving identity of the young label. 'It's modern, clean and very tonal with layers of texture created with our use of fabrics,' explains Sams of bassike's aesthetic. 'It's a contradiction in that the clothes always have a very understated and androgynous feel while remaining soft.' Inspired by the laidback Australian lifestyle, the designers believe cut and quality are key elements in their work.

Sams studied arts at university, majoring in Japanese language, but was inspired to work in the fashion industry after having worked in a retail store which sold labels such as Dries Van Noten and Yohji Yamamoto. Ryan, too, came from a different background, but found fashion a 'great way of expressing creativity,' becoming something she fell into. Meeting each other whilst working for Australian label Ksubi, the pair launched bassike in 2006. 'After many years working in the industry and travelling, the timing was perfect as we felt there was an opportunity to do something new.' bassike began with a concept: 'we developed our

1 (from left) Lurex singlet and jersey skirt; cotton shirt, S/S 09/10

own unique fabric and put a small collection together.' The collection, needless to say, was jumped on by leading retailers and media, building bassike a loyal following early on in their new venture. Today, the label is stocked in over 30 boutiques throughout Australia and New Zealand, as well as the brand's flagship store in Sydney. 'We hope that one day bassike is accessible in all parts of the world,' the designers add.

With this in mind, Sams and Ryan feel 'it is very important for us to have the right retail partners who will represent the brand in its entirety.' Having limited distribution to exclusive and selected stores, and opening their own retail store, bassike has been able to control its image and place in the market. Unique

in style and business manner, the use of organic materials on such a scale is, surprisingly, still a rare feat in an industry concerned with commercial value. 'We use organic cotton because it is our way of doing something positive for the environment,' the designers explain. 'It makes what we do a lot more complex and harder to produce, but it is an important aspect to us.' Such a process involves sourcing yarn and selecting fabric finishes to support the brand's individuality. This process ensures all shrinkage is removed from of the fabric so as customers can easily wash and wear the clothing continuously.

While it seems not the most conventional style of business, Sams and Ryan have been clever in approaching an under-catered sector of the market, and in a socially conscious manner. But this pair isn't patting themselves on the back in a self-congratulatory manner because, simply, they're doing what they love. 'We enjoy and are inspired by our work every day.'

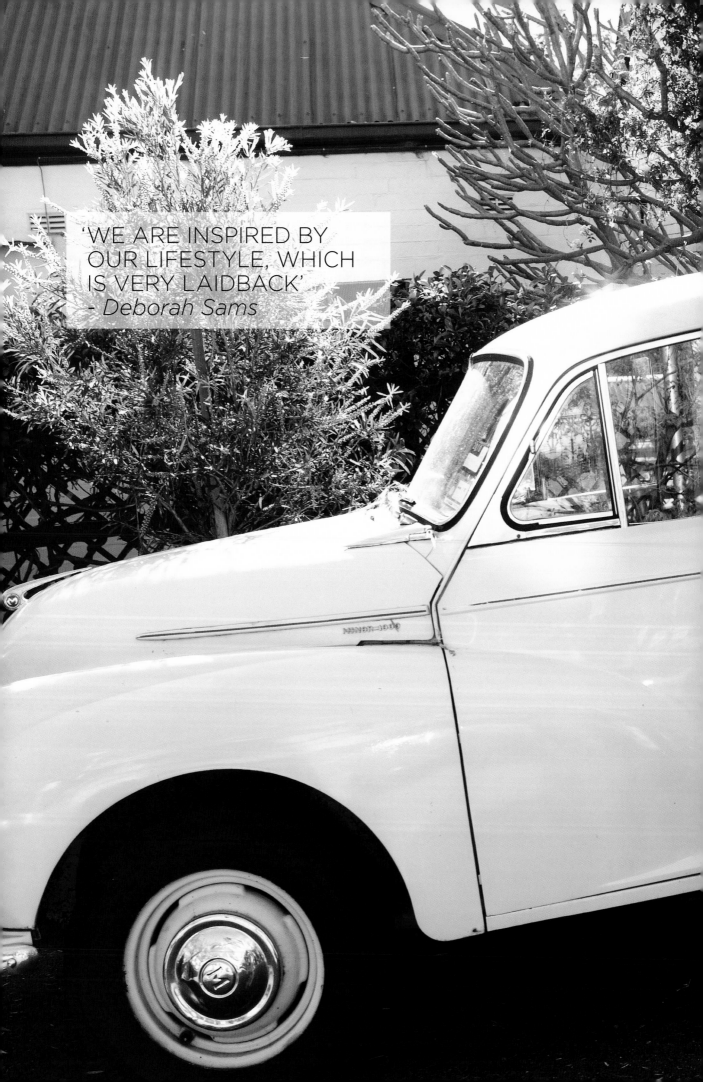

'WE ARE INSPIRED BY
OUR LIFESTYLE, WHICH
IS VERY LAIDBACK'
- *Deborah Sams*

2 Cotton linen two-piece suit and
cotton jersey t-shirt, S/S 09/10

3 Sand-blasted silk dress, S/S 09/10

BEAT POËT
EDWARD BERTOUCH AND JAMES JOHNSON

Beat Poët is one of few Australian fashion labels dedicated solely to menswear. With such strong focus on this market – and, in particular, an intelligent understanding of concept, construction and commercialism – its designers, Edward Bertouch and James Johnson, have gained a growing reputation for their design ethos.

Their clothing, which isn't typically Australian in its style or form, does not have an overriding theme each season. 'We want to cut back down to the relevant classics of the wardrobe,' says Johnson. 'That really is the thrust of what we do. We sit down, look at what we wear every day, what we need every day, and what we need to get rid of. It isn't about making a big statement, it's more about making modern, clean, wearable pieces.' This single concept is in stark contrast to the vast majority of designers, who speak of inspirations that evolve into a story told through their clothing. It's not to say that the clothes of Beat Poët don't tell a story, for there is a strong narrative quality inherent in the collection (made more potent when pieces are worn together) but it gives the clothes a universal quality and distinct wearability. The concept of 'cutting back' referenced by the designers shouldn't be confused with minimalism either. As they tell, the concept of bringing their work back to a pure core is inspired by Russian artist Kazimir Malevich and his manifestos on art ('his idea of reducing everything back to a pure form'). 'We call ourselves reductionists,' adds Johnson. Each season, then, is more of a branding exercise, in that the same thread of reduction is explored. 'We're getting closer to what we're trying to say or present, and there are always ways of refining it, or reinterpreting it, of making it more comfortable.' That there isn't a strong definition between summer and winter seasons – it's here that the

1 Layered cotton t-shirt,
S/S 09/10

brand's Melbourne roots really show – doesn't put Beat Poët at a disadvantage. Rather, it allows them to present a strong idea with the time to explore and perfect it. 'It's a full year wardrobe, essentially.'

Clever, too, is the designers' approach to how they present their ideas, not aligning themselves with the luxury market, but producing their clothes with the notion of value and accessibility in mind. 'We don't want to use excessively luxurious fabrics, to indulge in silks and cashmeres. Instead, we use fabrics that are good enough to do what they have to do and are accessible,' says Johnson. The fabrics used in the production of Beat Poët are predominantly made up of natural fibres, with the occasional addition of a synthetic for stretch or comfort. 'We appreciate the place of luxury in the world, and of how much effort can go into a single garment,' notes

Bertouch. 'But for us it is not so relevant to how we live or want to live. That particular idea of luxury is not very modern, and I think we've appealed to like-minded guys who love the sleek or sharp aesthetic of luxury brands, but don't necessarily need it to be made of Egyptian cotton or silk cashmere with lambskin detailing.' As Johnson simply says, 'you can never enjoy a luxury piece because it has a museum quality to it, and you feel as though you need to make it last forever.'

Beat Poët's production is of impeccable quality. Bertouch and Johnson are responsible for creating all patterns, sourcing fabric and creating samples. 'We have that control over the cut,' says Bertouch. 'We are very pedantic about where a seam is placed and if it is to move just a few millimetres, or if a slight curve is added to a collar.' Pattern blocks are also

2 Wool and viscose coat, cotton shirt, embroidered polyester tie and sterling silver lapel chain, S/S 08/09

created new each time a garment is made, with each piece reassessed to ensure it addresses its purpose in the wardrobe. Beat Poët is also produced entirely in Sydney, giving the designers even more control over the finished result of their work. One particular manufacturer also happens to work closely with the Australian military, which for Bertouch and Johnson, seems like the most perfect route for their production. 'They make military uniforms, and so at the end of the day the customer doesn't need to pay a huge amount of money for a garment, but it is obvious in the detail that the manufacturer is obsessed with construction,' says Bertouch. 'The pieces they make need to be strong and last a very long time. This is far more suited to our way of design as opposed to finding a luxury manufacturer in Europe.'

Bertouch and Johnson both grew up on Sydney's North Shore where they attended high school together. Johnson, having earned a bachelor degree at Sydney's College of Fine Arts, moved to Melbourne in 2005 to begin an internship with an Australian streetwear label. It was in Melbourne that he and Bertouch were to meet again, as Bertouch had left his Sydney-based degree in psychology to study at Melbourne School of Fashion, where he was taught patternmaking and construction. According to Bertouch, 'it was more of a hobby when we started working together. We were both studying or working a lot, and really didn't know many people, and it just evolved slowly, first with a small accessories range and later with clothes. Being in Melbourne as opposed to Sydney gave us the time and space to launch our full collection properly.' James adds that he and Bertouch 'spent a year working on the first collection and what they wanted the brand to be.'

The Spring/Summer 2009/2010 season was the first to be picked up by department store David Jones,

3 Cotton, polyester and spandex jacket, cotton trousers and canvas and leather messenger bag, S/S 09/10

'WE WANT TO CUT BACK DOWN TO RELEVANT CLASSICS OF THE WARDROBE' – *James Johnson*

4 Linen coat, cotton shirt, viscose tie and silicon solar panel brooch, S/S 09/10

which had been discussed for over four seasons but 'hadn't felt right.' 'David Jones have had really good representation of international brands,' says Bertouch, 'but until recently not so with local. They have bought a few other brands that sit alongside us, and have really understood our brand, buying a strong cross-section that represents what we do.' The David Jones inclusion could be attributed in part to Beat Poët's showing at Australian Fashion Week, the only individual menswear show of the event in 2009. And, while initially hesitant about the context of a catwalk for their brand's premise, the designers agree it was a great experience for them and the brand, resulting in considerable press coverage and increased sales. That success aside, Bertouch and Johnson have other plans for the future. 'I think our brand gets lost in the Australian scene, which tends to shout statements a lot, but we're happy going under the radar,' says Johnson. 'It is a really good test market for selling overseas, which, in the future, is probably where the brand has to go, and we've always known that.'

BETTINA LIANO
BETTINA LIANO

The name Bettina Liano is synonymous with Australian fashion. As one of the few labels that sparked growing public interest in local fashion designers in the late 1980s – alongside Peter Morrissey, Martin Grant and Alannah Hill – the Bettina Liano brand today continues to represent the epoch, remaining relevant to a broad, ageless audience, both locally and internationally.

Best known for her hipster skinny leg jeans ('made famous for fitting like a glove without being overly tight,' says Liano), the designer of the self-titled label explains that her brand was borne simply out of necessity. 'I needed money to survive,' explains Liano, 'and the situation to create something arose from necessity. I knew at once I should pursue this and nothing else. I was ambitious, and wanted to be able to look after myself. ' After creating a one-off dress for herself and selling it to a small Melbourne boutique, a cycle developed whereby Liano would use the money from each sale to buy more fabric, making another two. 'It wasn't a collection as such,' she adds jokingly. 'It was just me on the sewing machine, which I taught myself to use. Although one of the attractions of being a fashion designer was being surrounded by clothes and never not having anything to wear.'

In 1985, Liano submitted a folio of sketches in application of a show the (then) Fashion Design Council were putting together in Melbourne, which at the time was subsidised by the government. 'It was like *Project Runway* without the TV!' she exclaims. Alongside Morrissey, Grant and Fiona Scanlan, Liano showed to successful acclaim, shortly after opening a store (Sempre L'Unico) in Toorak Village, Melbourne, which she shared

1 Jersey and viscose dress, A/W 07

2 Stretch denim jeans, A/W 07

3 Cotton voile shirt, stretch denim dress and stretch denim jeans, S/S 09/10

with the above designers and others. While Liano's private life sped quickly (marrying, having her first child, falling out with her retail partner and mother), so too did her business, opening the first fully-branded Bettina Liano store in Toorak Village, before moving to Chapel Street in 1989. Responsible for this surge in growth, and in part for Liano's current position in the market, were her phenomenally successful velvet, button-fly jeans.

Although Liano and partner Roy Christou split in 1995, she continued to expand her business as a result of its popularity, becoming the sole managing director, creative director and head designer.

Such growth over two decades has positioned Bettina Liano comfortably in the domestic market with strong global exposure. As well as being stocked internationally, Liano maintains eight independent stores and is stocked nationally in department store Myer. Despite the success, Liano's focus remains firmly on the product she presents each season. 'I think about what my daughters and I want to wear, and that provides the most inspiration. There is a style that remains – you've got to have a signature style – but there are new ideas each season. I like servicing people; nothing makes me happier than when a woman is happy wearing my clothes. It's about making people feel good and not just taking their money. You need to service them with design, form, functionality and quality. The clothes should not fall apart and they should be styled so that they last. There is a classic element to them.' This in mind, it makes sense that the customer base of Bettina Liano is as extensive as the collections that she presents, which are 'designed with the female form in mind. I try to have something for everyone and make clothes that flatter different body shapes.'

Liano's collections are distinctly recognised by their large denim component, each garment adorned with a yellow flag. This style was so popular that fake versions appeared in the late 1990s, leading to the design being copyrighted. The collections also include dresses, skirts, shirts and suits, as well as belts, bags and shoes, which stylistically complement the apparel. 'I really love denim,' admits the designer. 'But I also love silk and leather... and I really like jersey. I've always had a passion for jersey,

even as it experienced a lull and now is back in style.' Remaining true to her own vision and identity has seen Liano ride successfully through dips in the market and overcome any hardships in the fashion industry. This she attributes largely to her passion and determination, which remain as strong as when she began creating clothes on her dining room table. 'I had nowhere to turn and it was like grains of sand in those first years. But I would say to myself that I would have a fashion empire because I really believed in what I was doing. It wasn't a power thing to say this, it was just an elevation from all that was going on in my life and making a choice about my future.' This sense of aspiration remains firmly central to the designer's creative vision, evident in the imagery she creates on a seasonal basis. 'I'm a highly visual person, and I love nothing more than to create a feeling, and give people a feeling.'

Liano is not content where she is today. Not that she isn't proud of her success, but she 'wouldn't mind diversifying into men's or children's wear one day. I've done a big retail expansion, so I'll wait a few years. I want to make my business a well-oiled machine with a strong foundation, not just a rack of clothes in a shop.'

'I'M NEVER
SATISFIED. IT'S
THE PLIGHT
OF AN ARTIST,
STRIVING TO
ACHIEVE MORE'
– *Bettina Liano*

4 Denim bodice and knit pants, A/W 07

BIRTHDAY SUIT
TECHA NOBLE, EMMA PRICE AND KATIE PRICE

As interview subjects, the designers of Birthday Suit – Techa Noble and sisters Emma and Katie Price – pose a challenge. While their product is essentially rooted in commercialism, the very basis of fashion business, the expressive output of their work has a much broader artistic value. Borne from their decade-old performance group, The Kingpins, Birthday Suit is a complex mode of conversation that explores the varying elements of costume: gender, culture, sexuality and race; those which subvert traditional ideas of beauty and challenge perceptions of the norm.

Founded in 2007, in association with their business partner Stefanos Stefanou, Birthday Suit remains intrinsically connected to their art practice. 'It always harks back to costume,' explains Emma. 'What we end up making is conceptually driven, but is often informed by something we find – a readymade wig or costume, for example. In a way, this creates a more complex conversation because what we make is inspired by something of the same medium.' In the same way that The Kingpins use dress to critique or put forward an alternative to the social norm, Birthday Suit is another 'tool in our kit, and we pull it apart and make it more abstract.' With this in mind, it seems obvious that these designers are not affected by their own product. Instead, they treat it with caution and thought.

'For me, fashion was always about dressing up,' explains Emma. 'I have a nostalgic approach to fashion, as opposed to perhaps a forward approach. It's collective. It's from a memory and of a time – an aesthetic of a particular era. We don't look at a trend – that from the onset has been my attraction to fashion and clothing.' This is the singular antithesis

'WHAT CAME OUT OF DRAG – AND DRAG FOR US ISN'T JUST A GENDER THING, IT'S NOT JUST A MAN DRESSED UP AS WOMAN OR VICE VERSA, IT HAS A MUCH BROADER SOCIAL PERFORMATIVITY TO IT – IS THAT APPEARANCE CAN BE AMPLIFIED AND THINGS CAN BE INFORMATIVE'
– Emma Price

of the concept of fashion for the majority of designers in the commercial world. While fashion references the past cyclically, it rarely acknowledges the present as a product of its history. For Noble, too, trends aren't on her radar. 'I was drawing before I could talk, and the first drawings I did were of costumes.' Although she notes her childhood obsession with (fashion designer) Sally Browne, Noble recalls her youth as surrounded by costume parties. 'I sometimes look at fashion and costume,' says Emma, 'and wonder whether they are the same thing.'

The Price sisters together part-own Sydney vintage emporium Zoo, whilst Noble works as a graphic artist, often in the fashion industry. To launch their own fashion label then seemed like a natural progression. And while adjunct to their art practice, the three are keen to create artistic delineation.

1 Silk top with beaded detail, satin and Lycra skirt, S/S 08/09

'WE HAVE OUR OWN HANDWRITING AND
WE AREN'T DOING WHAT EVERYONE ELSE IS.
EVEN OUR SUITING DOESN'T FOLLOW
THE CONVENTIONAL TEMPLATE OR TRENDS'
– *Brent Wilson*

3 Cotton shirt and
cotton singlet, A/W 09

personality and one's own style,'
offers the designer. Suiting may
be what Wilson is known for,
but it is his more casual offerings
that are at once more accessible
and affordable for the customer.

'It's called The Basics because it
consists of basics for men, including
t-shirts, singlets, shirting and
knitwear in ten colourways.
It is all well-cut and refined, just like
Brent Wilson pieces. There are a lot
of trickier pieces in the main range,
but the fit and fabrication remains
in The Basics, which separates it
from other labels.' Because, as
Wilson tells, the refined style of cut
and use of quality materials remains
similar to that of his suiting, the
clothes can be mixed dependent on
one's own style.

'A lot of people are doing a lot
of the same stuff,' believes the
designer of the menswear available
in the Australian market. 'They
follow trends and end up with a
similar silhouette and colour palette
– you can go into any store and
they are pretty much on par with
each other. Internationally, there
are great labels and they have
their own unique handwriting.'
It is Wilson's individual signature
that distinguishes his clothing and
explains his steady success in the
slow-moving menswear market.

The coming years won't see
the designer move rapidly into
womenswear or other ventures,
planning instead to focus on
Australia and the men's market,
seeing no point trying to do
everything at once. 'I'm interested
in setting the benchmark for
menswear in Australia, and then
going into the next phase,' tells
Wilson, unsure as yet what that
phase will be. 'I'm happy with what
I'm doing right now. It's great to be
doing everything but unless you're
consistent there is no point.'

4 Cotton singlet, denim jeans, wool
scarf and leather shoes, A/W 09

CAMILLA AND MARC
CAMILLA FREEMAN-TOPPER AND MARC FREEMAN

Camilla Freeman-Topper, one half of label camilla and marc with her brother Marc Freeman, won a competition held amongst her graduating class at fashion college. This win, she tells, sparked interest from the heads of Australian Fashion Week who invited her to show the collection at their next event. It was then that the wildly popular, on-trend brand was born.

The course Camilla was referring to was at the Whitehouse Institute of Design in Sydney, after which she earned a Masters degree at the Academia Arte Moda in Florence, Italy. Her brother Marc had studied a Bachelor of Engineering and Commerce at UNSW. Together, with Camilla's creative flair and technical design knowledge and Marc's business experience, creating a label seemed most fitting of their talents. 'Fashion was what I dreamed of doing from as far back as I can remember,' says Camilla. 'I asked Marc if he was interested in starting a brand – camilla and marc – and he was. We have different strengths and skills, so we balance each other very well.'

The camilla and marc aesthetic is one of binaries: frothy silk strapless dresses of billowing proportions paired with razor-cut, slick black leather jackets; belted bandage mini-dresses with slouchy, low-cut blazers with shawl collars. Evident in each collection, however, are elements of simplicity, elegance and luxury. The former is most prevalent in the label's typical use of a neutral, chalky colour palette of creams, light pinks, whites and greys, and the latter through the use of soft-washed leather, silks, cashmere and jersey, constructed with the contrasting use of draping and tailoring. 'Each of our collections is varied and evolved,' says Camilla, 'but those elements remain constant.'

1 Linen mix dress and jacket, A/W 10

2 Denim jeans, A/W 10

ruled by it. 'She has the ability to make smart decisions when it comes to style, allowing herself to indulge every now and then whilst knowing the value of practicality,' says Camilla. And it seems that this elusive customer provides camilla and marc a point of inspiration, too. 'Our summer collections are always influenced by the easy, natural way that Australians dress for summer,' she says, adding that 'we like our summer collections to feel and look fresh and have an elegant simplicity. For winter it's all about keeping it elegant but turning up the warmth and layers, so working with the most luxurious, comfortable and sophisticated fabrics possible.'

Stocked throughout Australasia, camilla and marc established a strong reputation and client following before opening their first store in Sydney's Paddington in 2009, which Camilla tells 'was a long-held dream for Marc and I. The store allows us to show the collections in their entirety and also brings us into close contact with our customers. It's also been very special to have the opportunity to express a complete vision of camilla and marc in terms of the design of the boutique.' Their following, they believe, is in large part due to the brand's presence at Australian Fashion Week, which 'has brought

The pair believe their customer is strong and self-assured; appreciative of their aesthetic and conscious of fashion but not

'WE HAVE
FOUND OTHER
DESIGNERS ARE
VERY SUPPORTIVE
OF THEIR PEERS,
REGARDLESS OF
COMPETITION'
*– Camilla Freeman-
Topper*

3 Lace dress,
A/W 10

4 Leather jacket and
cotton pants, A/W 10

us into contact with media and buyers and also helped us hone and develop our vision for the label.' In this environment, too, the pair finds the encouragement, advice and criticism of media, buyers and designers very useful and greatly appreciated.

With each season, camilla and marc aims to add a new element to the brand to add depth and longevity to their business, with newer lines including swimwear, denim and accessories. 'It's very exciting for us to be able to constantly add depth to an ever-expanding collection,' says Camilla. It is their goal to offer the camilla and marc customer a complete look and lifestyle.

5 Ponte dress, A/W 10

CARL KAPP

CARL KAPP

Carl Kapp's experience is as varied and rich as his work is today for his label of the same name. Born in South Africa and educated at the Natal Technikon in Durban, Kapp worked his way up from patternmaker in his first job to freelance creative design positions with Kenzo, Donna Karan and Trent Nathan, affording him the skill and expertise to launch his own label in Australia in 2006. Elegant and completely luxurious in its simplicity and fabrication, Kapp's contemporary work has found its way into the wardrobes of Cate Blanchett, Nicole Kidman and Rose Byrne, and most recently won him the 2009 Chambord Shine Award.

Kapp is thankful for the experience of working with such well-known international designers. 'It was purely creative and I didn't have to worry about production, and of course it was great being in Europe and America,' he tells. Having now set up his business in Sydney, away from the hype of Europe or the USA, Kapp uses the relative isolation to his advantage, finding no interest in trends overseas, but instead working organically in his studio by draping fabric on his mannequin and 'letting it happen'. 'I like clean, simple things, but they are often the hardest things to make because every single little detail will show,' says Kapp. The pieces that the designer suggests are not only his glamorous evening dresses – like his award-winning asymmetric 1930s-inspired gown in effervescent purple silk – but also his suiting. Hand-finished on the body or mannequin, the mastery of Kapp's tailoring is evident in the way the female form is shaped, which is at once classically beautiful and contemporary. And it is in the cut of Kapp's clothes – the way a suit is nipped in ever-so-slightly in the back to avoid any pouching, or the way a dress falls around the feet to create the effect of elegance – that lies the secret of his ability.

2 Print from S/S 09/10

1 Textured silk dress, A/W 09

The results embody a unique simplicity that suggests something about Kapp's ability to create elegant clothing through subtlety as opposed to grandeur.

Despite Kapp's penchant for cleanliness, his design studio is the archetypal creative space: messy and filled with his work, both works-in-progress and complete. 'Sorry about the space,' Kapp says apologetically when a visitor enters. 'We were going to clean up before you came but ran out of time,' he says, pointing to a vacuum cleaner buried beneath pattern off-cuts

and rolls of unused silk in a dazzling colour palette. Housed in an art-deco building within Sydney's Potts Point – the area where Kapp's work is most lauded due to its availability at luxury boutique Becker Minty, and his own Paddington store, opened in 2009 – the nature of his studio belies the beauty created within. The popularity of Kapp's formalwear only hints at legion of followers of his label, particularly popular – perhaps due to his geographical location – with high-powered and sophisticated businesswomen. His suiting defies any remaining bastion of the iconic 1980s power suit, where instead soft lines – created through the use of soft wools, Japanese-style collars and hand-stitched piping on edges – sculpt the female figure in a flattering, hourglass silhouette.

To watch Kapp work, as his well-established clients are allowed to do, unveils a mastery rarely seen in

3 Wool flannel and silk
hooded dress and patent
leather belt, A/W 09

4 Silk dress and patent leather belt, S/S 09/10

modern production. 'I understand the female figure, and create all of the patterns myself. If you know how the garment works and how it is put together, then you can do much more with it. You know what works,' says Kapp. This, coupled with the designer's obvious penchant for luxuriously soft and tactile fabrics, explains his ability to seduce the wearer.

Having been interested in fashion since childhood, the designer launched his own label in a bid for creative freedom. 'You're always going to have to answer to other people, but now it's my vision and the only person I answer to is my customers.' Carl Kapp is manufactured entirely in Australia, and the designer's studio houses a few staff that work as cutters and machinists. Since launching, Kapp has gained several stockists in Australia and in 2008 set up an online store to cater for customers living interstate or overseas.

Kapp's intention is to maintain a high standard of quality and grow the business steadily in response to demand. As he notes, 'people in Australia are more careful about what they're buying today and they can't be fooled. There are so many brands that have a lot of hype surrounding them, which is great, but you really need to have the quality to sell through and follow on with the next season. It's a fine balance of creating outstanding pieces and getting the coverage to promote it, which is why we're doing things slowly; we want to ensure it's right each season.' It is an idea that resonates with the designer's view of what constitutes success, which he believes does not come from money or fame. 'When you look back at a finished collection, that's what keeps you going; it is what has killed you for six months and so if you don't get a kick out of what you're doing it wouldn't be worth it.'

5 Silk dress with tie-back belt, S/S 09/10

'I DRAW A COLLECTION AFTER IT'S FINISHED, NEVER BEFORE; IT ALL HAPPENS ON THE MANNEQUIN, AND THAT'S REALLY HOW IT WORKS. YOU JUST LET IT HAPPEN AND SEE WHERE IT GOES'
– Carl Kapp

6 Print from S/S 09/10

CHRØNICLES ØF NEVER
GARETH MOODY

When one writes about fashion it is often too easy to describe visual elements of a garment, be it texture, cut or colour, as opposed to the meaning behind it. For the work of Gareth Moody, such limited descriptions don't work – all we would know about CHRØNICLES ØF NEVER is that it is made of high-quality black fabrics in unconventional patterns and utilitarian styles. And yet, beyond this, CHRØNICLES ØF NEVER evokes a sense of calm and peace, of dreams and unlimited imagination, be that of Moody himself or of the life his clothes take on once worn.

Before creating his own label in 2006, Moody was one of the three original designers of cult Australian denim label Ksubi (then Tsubi) that existed at this stage as a mish-mash of creative ideas, having not yet established its singular design vision, nor realised its own commercial potential. After leaving the trio, Moody took some time away from the world of fashion to redefine his design philosophy. He did so by creating a small capsule collection of jewellery, including unisex necklaces, bracelets and rings sculpted from brass, and brushed and blackened silver that acted as a prelude to the clothes that would later come. 'It was a break from my previous experience in the industry,' Moody tells of his early work under the name of CHRØNICLES ØF NEVER. 'I just needed to settle down a little bit and work out what I wanted to do and my own look.' Collections aside, this was Moody's most clever career decision, for when he finally launched a full collection of clothing there existed a language unique to CHRØNICLES ØF NEVER; a language that remains and has become, season after season, more refined and eloquent.

1 Modal t-shirt, cotton jacket, leather shorts and leather boots, S/S 08/09

2 Cotton jumper, wool vest and leather boots, S/S 08/09

Playing with the use of fundamental materials such as leather, knits, denim and cotton, Moody blends tailored and fluid silhouettes to create unisex collections that are seemingly inspired by mathematics and architecture in the way that they shape and surround the body. This play of proportions and fabrics – oftentimes narrow-leg shrunken denim jeans with oversized, unhemmed scalloped leather jackets, or drop-crotch pants in stretch cotton with wrinkled cotton narrow-cut, long-line collared shirts – poses an interesting interpretation of the human form and the way it can be aesthetically defined and refined. And yet despite the unusual proposition of shape, Moody employs the use of extremely traditional garments: white cotton collared business shirts, black wool waistcoats, denim jeans and lace-up leather shoes. This mutation of garments

'THE BRAND ISN'T GOING TO CHANGE CHARACTER NEXT SEASON; IT'S GOING TO HAVE THE SAME UNDERLYING THEME AND PERSONALITY'
– *Gareth Moody*

4 Cotton trench, A/W 07

fuels the thought process of Moody: constantly evolving age-old silhouettes and styles; and yet categorically distinguishing him from those who follow trends and regurgitate seasonal styles.

It is obvious Moody believes in his own work. He notes that 'the aesthetic is still apparent today, two years later, and it still has a nice reception.' And thankfully he has no plans to radically alter the underlying theme of his work, as much as trends may change. 'The customers have begun to recognise the aesthetic and style. I don't chop and change with the seasons. The brand isn't going to change character next season; it's going to have the same underlying theme and personality. Perhaps it's my personality. It just feels nice.' Having grown organically and slowly as a business, it's a mantra that fits well.

As well as clothes and jewellery, Moody has also introduced shoes, which he manufactures in Indonesia, and eyewear, on which he collaborates with Graz Mulcahy. As a complete look, CHRØNICLES ØF NEVER remains consistent and yet at the same time each category stands up as its own entity. The strength of these lines lies in Moody's choice of collaborators, people he has worked with in the past. 'They're now keyed back into this business for the right reasons,' he says. 'And it hasn't been all at once.'

With such a strong identity, Moody is able to work on diffusion and capsule projects with retailers, such as *Black Noise, White Rain* with General Pants Co., without sacrificing his creative integrity. Consisting of footwear, denim and shirts, the diffusion line provides

3 Cotton jumper, wool vest and
leather boots, A/W 07

5 Wool jumper, wool poncho and leather boots, A/W 09

6 Leather jacket, cotton shirt, cotton metal pants and leather boots, A/W 09

the CHRØNICLES ØF NEVER label access to a different sector of the market. 'Because we import a lot of high quality fabric and leathers, and all of our product is made in Australia, the prices are justifiably increasing. This capsule collection uses simple cottons and observes the reality of the marketplace. The main line is quite exclusive in a way, and we don't want to bastardise it [for price point], and so we can play with the diffusions.' This type of project is a more suitable exhibition of Moody's work as opposed to a runway event. 'People can get a real understanding of what it is, and it's a special process which makes it fun for the public.'

At the heart of various ventures and special projects remains Moody's defined vision and belief in the strength of his brand. 'I'm very particular with all of that,' he says of CHRØNICLES ØF NEVER's identity. 'I had time to figure out all of those things.'

7 Leather jacket, cotton singlet, leather shorts and leather boots, S/S 09/10

8 Modal t-shirt and cotton blazer, S/S 09/10

COLLETTE DINNIGAN
COLLETTE DINNIGAN

Her sparkly cocktail dresses may be synonymous with red carpet celebrities, but designer Collette Dinnigan is much more than a dresser of the stars. In fact, her many achievements make her a star in her own right. Stocked in the world's most prestigious stores including Barney's and Harvey Nichols, as well as her own boutiques, Dinnigan has forged a name for herself through tireless dedication to her art over the past two decades. Most recently she was invited to join the committee of the Chambre Syndicale – the French fashion industry governing body – which is a much-lauded accolade for any designer in the world.

As Dinnigan explains, she was involved with the art scene growing up and had access to her mother's work as a textile designer, where she learnt to sew. 'I originally wanted to study veterinary science or marine biology, but was very creative and so chose fashion instead.' Dinnigan trained at the Wellington Polytechnic in New Zealand and then worked in the costume department of the ABC in Sydney and as head costume designer for several films. When funding of the Australian film industry was cut and jobs dried up, Dinnigan launched her own label with the first collection being produced in 1990. Her background in costume design might explain the glamorous nature of her work today, most loved by celebrities for red carpet events.

Gaining several international stockists in her initial years as a designer, Dinnigan established a global presence and began staging annual ready-to-wear fashion shows in Paris in 1995 and today remains the only Australian designer invited to do so by the Chambre Syndicale. 'We're still stocked in the same stores; I think longevity is a key factor in success.

Your work might be bought by great stores but if you can't sustain the sales you disappear quickly because the stores are so key to your distribution.' While Dinnigan understood the principles of good business, it was still a challenge to overcome the language and cultural barriers that working within a global market presented. 'Most people didn't even know where Australia was when I started selling to Barney's in the early nineties,' she jokes. 'Though as time has gone by our local fashion events and movie stars have put Australia on the map.' It is interesting here that in Dinnigan's experience in foreign countries, it is Australia's cultural progression that has made the country as recognisable and well-known as it is today.

1 Silk georgette and sequin top and wool Lycra tuxedo pants with beading, A/W 08

Dinnigan set the bar for the slowly developing Australian fashion industry early on. Taking inspiration from exotic tales, the designer creates a clever hybrid of old and new ideas each season.

2 Silk georgette dress with metallic sequins and ostrich feathers, A/W 08

'I like mixing things that are contrasting: something feminine with the androgynous; something 1930s with something completely futuristic.' What holds the Collette Dinnigan aesthetic together is the continued signature of quality in the clothing. 'A teenage girl might be wearing her mother's old Collette Dinnigan printed dress from 15 years ago, but the clothes have a timeless elegance and can be worn for years. My work is not disposable by any means.' A selection of Dinnigan's most significant pieces were featured in the Victoria & Albert Museum's *Fashion In Motion* exhibition in London in 2000, including her exquisite hand-beaded eveningwear for which she is internationally famed.

As a businesswoman, Dinnigan has seen the same success as her designs. Some of her honours include the 1997 Louis Vuitton Business Award; and the 2008 National Retailers' Association Award for Fashion Excellence.

For Dinnigan, the most notable accolade was being invited to join the Chambre Syndicale. As she tells, 'it is one thing to show in Paris every season, but I still didn't even think they knew my name.' In this role she meets with key international fashion figures to ensure the successful development of fashion through events such as Paris Fashion Week and education initiatives.

The imminent future will see continued focus on her retail business, though Dinnigan does not plan to expand in any other way than continuing to develop her product. 'I'm trying to focus on creating tighter collections, on producing more haute couture, rather than spreading myself too thin.' There is often a lot to manage, admits the designer, claiming that she 'would love to take some time to smell the roses, though it's nice to dream of this and remain designing rather than the other way around.'

'I THINK
LONGEVITY IS
A KEY FACTOR
IN SUCCESS'
– *Collette
Dinnigan*

3 Stretch polyamide camisole with elastane lace
trim g-string, Wild Hearts by Collette Dinnigan for
Marks & Spencer, UK, 2002

CYBÈLE

Many a fashion magazine has overused the word 'feminine' to describe anything frilly, floaty or pastel in colour. The collections of Cybèle are feminine, but in a more modern sense that appeals to the intelligence of the New Zealand label's customer and the way she buys clothes to reflect her personality and confidence. The bold, graphic clothes are a strong addition to a woman's wardrobe.

'I think of my customer as wise and savvy, with an eye for detail and difference,' says designer Cybèle Wiren from her Auckland studio. Wiren herself embodies such qualities, which are reflected in her original clothing, designed and cut to empower a woman and make her feel sexy in luxurious materials. Not distracted by obvious trends, Wiren custom-designs the label's prints herself, and uses them in clever combinations of pattern. Having majored in painting in her visual communications degree at Unitec in Auckland, it makes sense that print forms a large part of the Cybèle aesthetic. As she explains, 'the design process usually starts with the colour palette and textiles, and evolves from there. I draw on any and all aspects of the world around me: natural elements, history, characters and stories.'

Dreaming as a child to become 'all sorts of things', including an architect, scientist and lawyer, Wiren did not consider a career in fashion until the end of her degree, but had made clothes 'from the age she could reach the sewing machine pedal.' During her study, Wiren worked in several fashion-related jobs, such as screen printing and sample machining, and took night classes in patternmaking in Melbourne upon graduating. 'I contracted to a number of companies, and also worked as a design

'I THINK OF MY
CUSTOMER
AS WISE AND
SAVVY, WITH
AN EYE FOR
DETAIL AND
DIFFERENCE'
– *Cybèle Wiren*

1 Silk dress, S/S 08/09

2 Silk dress, S/S 08/09

room assistant for Tina Borg, which involved creating spec sheets for offshore production.' In 2003 Wiren directed her creative energy into creating her first collection of eight pieces in the front room of her shared flat. The clothes, which sold to a considerable number of four stores, provided her with the motivation to create a second collection. 'It's grown every season since then,' she says.

Now sold throughout New Zealand, Australia and Asia, Wiren shows her collections annually as part of New Zealand Fashion Week, and also through showrooms in Auckland, Sydney and Tokyo, allowing for greater international sales reach. In 2007, Wiren was a finalist in the Bayer Innovators Award, held in association with The National Business Review, which pre-empted her winning the Air New Zealand Export Award the following year. 'I have received a lot of support from within the industry,' she explains, 'though in terms of business the ultimate responsibility comes back to me. Every season brings developments in new markets, special projects and collaborations to explore.' That said, Wiren's favourite moment is the excitement of seeing a collection brought to life on a runway.

3 Silk dress, S/S 08/09

DHINI
DHINI PARARAJASINGHAM

Dhini Pararajasingham, the designer behind self-titled label Dhini, is fascinated by tailoring and haute couture, her signature in the Australian fashion industry. Pararajasingham's expertise is a result of extensive training – both technical and experiential – providing her with a distinct point of difference.

Pararajasingham originally worked in marketing where, over time, she gained the confidence to pursue her love of fashion. 'Fashion was something I wanted to do since I was five years old,' she tells. 'I was always drawing dresses and shoes, but growing up I got sidetracked and didn't have the confidence to go into fashion.' Before training at the highly demanding fashion course at RMIT University, Melbourne, Pararajasingham studied a technical foundation course in Tokyo, Japan. RMIT, she tells, 'is one of the best training grounds to move straight into the industry.' True to her word, Pararajasingham was recognised by renowned Melbourne boutique Alice Euphemia with the Most Promising Student Award for her graduate collection, with the boutique holding an exhibition of her work during L'Oreal Melbourne Fashion Festival in 2004.

During her study, Pararajasingham worked with eminent Australian bridal designer Mariana Hardwick, gaining valuable skills in tailoring, couture construction and detailing. It was this experience that led her to work with a tailor and couturier for her graduate collection. And, later in 2004, Pararajasingham relocated to London where she worked as Design Assistant and Production and Manufacturing Assistant for the inimitable label Boudicca. Here, she assisted the designers in producing their collection for London and Paris Fashion Weeks. 'Working for

1 Rayon and
polyester dress,
A/W 10

Boudicca was incredible, and that experience is what equipped me to start my own label. They had accepted me for their internship position and it was crazy: seven-day weeks, fourteen-hour days. I was thrown into the deep end. I had to do everything from patterns, to cutting samples, to sewing, to creating accessories for the show. I proved that I was the most competent of the interns because I was promoted.' However after a year, with no room for upward promotion, Pararajasingham left and launched her own label.

In the capacity of her own label, Pararajasingham showed her first collection as part of London Fashion Week. 'It's not like Australia,' she tells. 'There is a longer process you have to go through, and new labels don't tend to go straight into showing on schedule, anyhow.' In 2006, Pararajasingham based herself in Melbourne once again, launching domestically with a show at Australian Fashion Week to high acclaim.

Pararajasingham's work, unlike many, is inspired by clothing design and genre as opposed to something intangible. 'That's my signature,' she agrees. 'When I started in 2004, I saw a gap in the market for a craft-like aesthetic of details. In a way it's about pushing boundaries in form, detail and structure.

2 Viscose and cotton jacket, cotton top, cotton and spandex jeans, and wool felt hat with tassles and ribbons, S/S 09/10

'I SAW A GAP IN THE MARKET FOR A CRAFT-LIKE AESTHETIC OF DETAILS... IT'S ABOUT PUSHING BOUNDARIES IN FORM, DETAIL AND STRUCTURE' – *Dhini Pararajasingham*

'My training taught me to be conceptual in the way my design starts and finishes.' Pararajasingham extensively researches, references and bases her collections on styles of clothing – such as marching band uniforms or eighteenth-century men's tailoring – and interprets them in a modern, relevant manner that still honours the history and tradition of the concept.

'I love working with wools, because it lends itself well to my tailoring. But at the same time, I love working with techno fabrics and new developments. I try to contrast these classic and innovative fabrics to give that edge; to offer something new or different.' This is indeed evident in Pararajasingham's use of binary: cropped military jackets with epaulets and gold, hand-sewn rope detailing, paired with silk wool, high-waisted harem pants; or a high waisted, A-line skirt, contrasted in form and fabric with a silk blouse of billowing ruffles and sheer cross panels. This style, she tells, attracts an intelligent, creative customer. 'Someone that supports the concept of innovation, because that's what she wants to express about herself.'

3 Silk and tencel top, silk and
tencel harem pants and wool
felt hat with tassels, S/S 09/10

DION LEE
DION LEE

'The next big thing' is a much overused title in fashion, but it seems appropriate to make an exception for Dion Lee. At 22, Lee was selected as one of four students to show his graduation collection at Australian Fashion Week in 2008, and within days had editors photographing his conceptual, edgy pieces.

Lee's study at the TAFE Design Institute combined with his cool style sensibility has afforded him the opportunity to create desirable and unique clothing. As he explains, 'I have always wanted to be involved in some aspect of design, and when I was at high school this turned more and more into fashion as something I really wanted to explore.' As a designer, Lee hopes to continue 'doing creative things' while sustaining a business, which he manages entirely himself, from production through to marketing. 'I'd love to continue to grow and eventually move into the international market as it's quite small here.'

His first collection, part of the *Four Boys* show, comprising selected graduating students from the TAFE Design Institute, was received with rapturous applause. 'It's great to receive praise for what I've done but it doesn't necessarily make me think my work itself is great, and you're always most critical of your own work,' he says reflectively. One key audience member that was enthralled by Lee's work was Belinda Seper of The Corner Shop retail group, who instantly bought his collection for her stores. This sales outlet provided Lee with a platform to road-test his first collection in a live marketplace, upon which he developed ideas, cuts and methods of production.

'A LOT OF MY WORK COMES FROM THE DEVELOPMENT OF CUTS AND PLAYING WITH PATTERNMAKING – THE GARMENTS PLAY WITH PERCEPTION'
– Dion Lee

With the use of laser cutting, graphic manipulations, pleating and layering, Lee draws a sophisticated aesthetic that plays with perception. As he tells, 'there are no specific influences; my work comes from the development of cuts and playing with patternmaking.' The combination of such techniques presents a distinct aesthetic, part futuristic vision, part examination of the human form. Indeed, sharply sculptured dresses and jackets with cut-outs and experimental exaggeration make for an interesting and distinctly individual silhouette.

While known as the young designer du jour following his first collection, even more remarkable is Lee's consistent, well-structured and strong collection the following year, staged in the basement of a Kings Cross car park during Australian

1 Sheer pants, sheer tights, sound-absorbing polypropylene foam jacket, leather shoes, A/W 10

Fashion Week. Earning him international praise, the designer proved his ability to consistently produce work of a high standard, not only in terms of quality and production, but extending ideas explored in his previous work. Such a cool and considered response to the hype and pressure on the young designer's shoulders has earned him high respect in the Australian industry, where his clothes remain highly covetable.

2 Gazar skirt, cotton shirt, A/W 10

3 Wool dress
S/S 09/10

4 Wool dress
S/S 09/10

5 Leather skirt and silk
blouse, S/S 09/10

6 Leather skirt and
silk blouse, S/S 09/10

7 Jersey and cotton dress, and
leather shoes, S/S 09/10

8 Jersey and cotton
dress S/S 09/10

EASTON PEARSON
PAMELA EASTON AND LYDIA PEARSON

A 2009 exhibition of Easton Pearson's 21-year-history at the Gallery of Modern Art at the Queensland Art Gallery demonstrated the spectacular design, detail, influences and production of the designers' work. One of the largest individual exhibitions of an Australian fashion house, the exhibition exposed the mesh of cultures, ideas and techniques inherent in the collections, and how its artistic aesthetic has evolved, matured and mutated over the course of its history.

Designers, directors and friends Pamela Easton and Lydia Pearson commenced partnership and business in 1989, wanting to design together. The brand was first established as Bow and Arrow by Easton Pearson, followed by a diffusion, Oh! by Easton Pearson. 'After a little while, we just decided it was easier to call it Easton Pearson,' explains Pearson. Both interested in fashion and clothing from a young age, designing was not something either Easton or Pearson had considered as a serious career, and fell upon it, according to Pearson, 'by default, almost.' Pearson had created her own brand for ten years and Easton was working as a buyer when the pair decided to merge their interests. 'We came from different aspects of the industry but with similar interests and similar strengths.'

The designers showed their collections in Australia for a decade before moving their presentations to Paris in 1998. As Easton tells, 'we showed in Paris because international buyers wanted to see the next season, and we chose Paris because it was the most suitable place for us to show.' And although the brand stopped showing at Australian Fashion Week in 2002 as it didn't fit with their sales calendar (excluding 2008 to celebrate their twentieth year in business), they believe that Australian Fashion

1 Dip-dyed silk dress with cotton thread bodice, S/S 08/09

'THERE IS A VERY ARTISANAL FEEL TO THE CLOTHING WE MAKE'
– Pamela Easton

Week is largely to thank for the success of today's local industry. 'When Australian Fashion Week first started, Australian fashion didn't have an export industry,' tells Pearson. 'Collette [Dinnigan] was selling in Paris, but she was one of the only ones before Simon Lock created the event. It really gave Australian designers that opportunity for export and to show their designs to the rest of the world. Australian Fashion Week was and is really important.' Today, Easton Pearson supplies over 100 stores in 24 countries worldwide, and maintains retail spaces in Sydney and Brisbane.

The designers explain that their way of working is inseparable from their design ethos, as they work in partnership through all passages of the design process: planning,

designing, finishing, travelling and selling. Central to the design and aesthetic of Easton Pearson is undoubtedly the use of textiles and embellishment. As Easton explains, 'We create about 90 percent of our textiles, or commission the weaving, the design of the prints, and other pieces. That's the beginning of the design.' Such textiles draw on the rich history of various cultures, from India to Africa, through to vintage clothes, museums, archives, literature and the designers' own travels. They explain that the possibilities offered by specific textile techniques influence them in terms of what might be adapted to clothing. Perhaps partly due to the geographic proximity of their Queensland base to Asia, Easton Pearson represents a melange of Asian Pacific cultures through a manifestation of techniques and fabrics and the relationships built through commerce.

India, the label's closest country in terms of development of their work,

2 Silk organza
dress, S/S 08/09

is represented in an Easton Pearson collection through the use of colour and embellishment; of lusciously vivid pinks, purples, yellows and blues in woven silks with hand-sewn beads, unhemmed calico, delicate cottons and diamante crystals. Each collection, an exploration of techniques and styles as much as themes and ideas, consists of an extensive range of garments: from simple day dresses to evening jackets, from ruffled feathered skirts to beaded singlet tops. In preparation for the design process, Easton and Pearson travel to various countries to work closely with its craftspeople in researching textile traditions. 'There is a very artisanal feel to the clothes we make,' says Easton. 'It's about decoration, colour and interesting construction. And we design with a lot of different 'someones' in mind. We definitely have a mythical muse that we invoke when we're working, but it's not a person because the clothes appeal to a lot of different ages, sizes and mindsets, and it can look very different when worn by different people. It seems the people attracted [to the clothing] are those that can make it their own.'

Essentially a ready-to-wear design house, Easton Pearson's employment of such intricate techniques, textiles and the limited size of production hint at the notion of haute couture. The designers believe in this regard that the clothes have relevance and longevity. 'I think if someone is going to invest in something that costs as much as the clothing we

3 Silk satin top and skirt, S/S 08/09

make does, they want longevity. You might put it away and find it irrelevant for five years, but when you discover it again it has something intrinsically beautiful about it,' says Easton. The brand produces three ranges each year: Spring/Summer, Cruise and Autumn/Winter, as well newly introduced diffusion line EP by Easton Pearson, and a manchester line which plays on the brand's relationship with textiles. The designers are also responsible for the financial support and overall direction of their business. As Pearson explains, 'we're still a very independent company and we still drive it every day.'

ELLERY
KYM ELLERY

Kym Ellery can, in large part, attribute the commercial success of her label Ellery to her experience in fashion publishing. Not that Ellery ever intended to work in magazines, she explains, but having worked as the market editor for indie fashion title *Russh* activated the 'styling part of the brain'; a knowledge and understanding of trends and combinations that she has been able to apply to her label since its launch in 2007.

Upon leaving school, Ellery studied fashion design and production in her hometown of Perth before moving to Sydney and later attended short courses in design and illustration at London's famed Central Saint Martins. 'I always had a great interest in art,' she explains, 'but fashion was my first love.' And yet before launching her brand, the only hands-on experience the designer had acquired was making things for herself. Launching the Ellery brand with a Spring/Summer collection, the young designer staged a show a week prior to the official Australian Fashion Week in a friend's Surry Hills art gallery which, she claims proudly, was a great success. 'I was very lucky and had lots of support starting out and still do,' she adds.

Ellery's keen eye for trends and her eclectic sources of inspiration (she notes Helmut Newton, Tracey Emin and Mario Testino as some of her artistic idols), results in a collection that she describes as 'fashion forward, bold and structural.' Such words depict something sci-fi and masculine, when in actuality Ellery's clothing has a distinct femininity to it in the way it is cut and shapes the body, creating hourglass silhouettes through the use of a cinched waist or a slimmed body line with an exaggerated shoulder. Adding to the individuality of Ellery's work is her love of developing fabrics, 'whether it be a print design or [as per her Spring/Summer 2010 season] a very detailed embroidered fabric. I am lucky to have a very talented mother who happens to be a textile designer. She is inspirational.' The embroidered fabric that Ellery refers to was used throughout the collection by way of blazers, low-cut singlet tops and v-shaped pants.

This specific collection, according to Ellery, was inspired by a YouTube clip of a Miss Teen USA competition of 1987; a film she describes as 'simply fabulous!' And, while not a direct representation of the event, prevalent was a range of peplum skirts in bronze metallic fabrics, singlets and tops in low-back leotard-style cuts and embellishment with ruffles, plaited tassels and faux-fur throughout. Fluffy, blown out high ponytails further communicated this idea, 'which is why I love shows,' explains Ellery. 'They tell a full story with the lights, music, hair and makeup. I want everything to tell a story and make sense as a whole.'

Showing at events such as Australian Fashion Week doesn't come without challenges for the young designer, noting that most recently she was the last scheduled show of the day, and with a day's worth of late shows, hers became very late indeed. 'There is also the added trial of sharing models between shows, but all in the name of fashion.' For the end result – a

1 Embellished crepe rayon top, brocade skirt and leather lattice boots, A/W 10

well-communicated vision to her customer – Ellery is happy to endure the stresses of staging a presentation. This customer, she tells, 'is very sure of her style. She is of no particular age or background, she just loves to look great and individual.' And, for the time being, Ellery is committed to continually developing her work so as to deliver a strong, well-made and relevant product – an effort she hopes will culminate in European distribution and greater exposure in the US market.

'In this industry you have to be both creative and business-savvy, which is tiring but you really have no choice. I think I am doing okay in that regard.' With a motto of 'onward and upward', it is little wonder that Ellery maintains the energy to juggle her various creative commitments and still successfully produce a trend-relevant collection each season.

'I THINK THAT THERE IS
NOTHING MORE BEAUTIFUL
THAN THE STRENGTH OF
THE FEMALE FORM'
– *Kym Ellery*

2 Embellished crepe rayon
top, wool-felt shorts and
leather lattice boots, A/W 10

3 Leather jacket, acid-washed
cotton t-shirt and
leather lattice boots, A/W 10

117

ELSOM
SAM ELSOM

'Sustainability is paramount,' says Sam Elsom. 'We are constantly on the search for new textiles and have gone to many lengths to create our own cloth in order to reach our quality expectations.' Working with cotton farmers in India, silk farmers in China and cotton mills in Italy, Elsom has built a fashion label with a social conscience. Mindful that green fashion won't translate to the mainstream if it remains corralled in a hippy ghetto of its own making, Elsom is as passionate about the aesthetics of fashion as he is about producing it with minimal environmental impact. Having started off selling organic t-shirts at markets, Elsom is now a fully-fledged fashion label that is sold in both small boutiques and department stores. 'Most important,' he says, 'is that we do it in a way that is clean, sophisticated and elegant.'

Elsom studied fashion design in London, at Central Saint Martins, as well as in Sydney, at FBI College, at the time that he began working in the fashion industry for mass label Bracewell. As Elsom tells, 'Bracewell was an amazing learning ground. The size of the brand meant that I was able to learn abut all aspects of fashion, including business.' While educational, perhaps the sheer size of Bracewell and its production was responsible for bringing environmental responsibility to Elsom's attention. While still working for Bracewell, he also began his t-shirt brand Found (which he still runs today), selling them at markets on weekends and eventually setting up a wholesale network. 'It was through [Found],' Elsom says, 'that I was exposed to the world of organic textiles and learned a lot about the process of production and the effect on the environment. However, I found that as a customer, just because you support organic textiles or sustainable farming doesn't mean you want to dress like Mahatma Gandhi.

1 S/S 07

have just begun
working with an
organic cloth
made from milk.' Elsom describes
the invention process with such
excitement and passion that its
easy to forget the challenges
posed, as well as the cost. But,
with a niche selection of stockists
around the globe, Elsom does not
have an aggressive growth strategy,
affording him the time and space to
experiment with manufacturing and
production processes. 'We manage
our sales in-house, and don't take
part in trade fairs or fashion weeks;
our main focus is on design and
delivering quality which exceeds
expectations. I believe in growing
slowly, and this allows us to iron out
the kinks as they approach.'

Elsom's collections, which consist
of laidback suiting, shirts, casual
separates and accessories, are
inspired by offbeat personalities,

The fact is there were few options
available, particularly for young
people.' Through research and with
the help of fair trade organisations,
the budding designer created
his own label with the mission of
changing the identity of organic
textiles and educating people on
the benefits of sustainable farming
and textile production.

That his product is organic remains
the core of Elsom's business, and
while it's a hurdle that most fashion
labels don't have to jump, it's
something that he feels strongly
about, learning new techniques and
processes as he goes. 'We have
worked with Italian mills who have
helped us develop these cottons
and silks into cloth. We have used
recycled plastic bottles to make
polyesters and sequins. And we

2 S/S 07

much like his customer. 'I don't have a muse as such, but inspiration comes from being outside my natural environment or breaking routine. Each season is a new perspective on Elsom... a new look for the same customer, but with the same clean aesthetic.' Elsom notes such artists as French poet Arthur Rimbaud as of interest to him, and one might expect Elsom's work, in years to come, to have the same enduring and pervasive influence on the state of fashion production.

Elsom believes that the only way to go in the future is up. 'I'd like to see us continue the ingenuity in sustainable textiles and keep pushing a high quality product. I believe we will always be a niche brand with a left-of-centre design direction, and I think ultimately whether you are into our design direction or not, there is a shift in environmental consciousness taking place.'

3 S/S 07

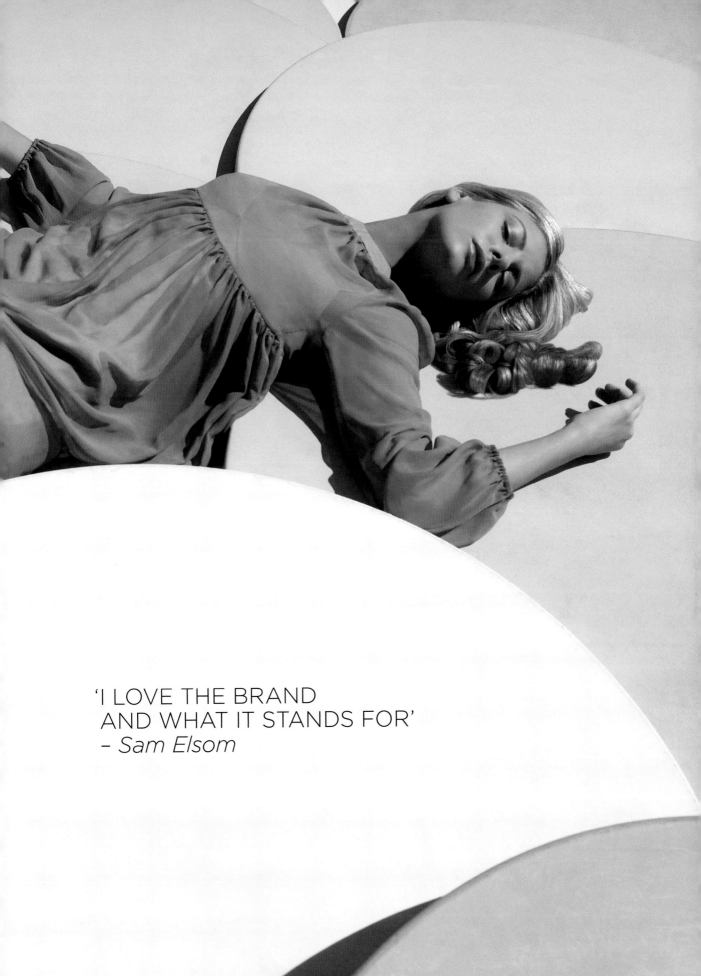

'I LOVE THE BRAND
AND WHAT IT STANDS FOR'
– *Sam Elsom*

FERNANDO FRISONI
FERNANDO FRISONI

Fernando Frisoni's current label was first created in a collaborative business with womenswear designer Nicola Finetti, resulting in two seasons of highly acclaimed work. After splitting to pursue individual creative ideas, Frisoni took some time to develop his new, independent label, which is growing slowly, naturally and humbly. His clothes are still characteristic of his work with Finetti, but are now more succinct and realised, and as such have greater viability for success.

While Frisoni hasn't sacrificed his distinctly unique aesthetic, his ideas have been cleverly shaped to more adequately respond to the needs and desires of the modern man; the customer who is still coming to terms with the concept of high fashion, and the increased price that often accompanies the quality of such work. While his Australian customer base might be quite small in actuality, Frisoni prefers to focus only on the imminent future, directing his energies on creating honest design, growing his creativity and understanding the market. 'I'd like to grow and sell much more around the world, but I'm humble about my wishes; the brand is young, and I have many years,' he explains.

In the fashion world Frisoni is at his most comfortable. 'I was born into it,' says the stylist-turned-designer. Since moving to Australia from Brazil, Frisoni worked as a sartorial street photographer for the *Sun-Herald,* his column gaining a cult following as he captured the outfits of everyday people. 'Usually when people are walking in the streets they have two extremes: on-trend or innovative. I'm interested in what people are wearing on the streets – these are the people who buy your clothes, and while fashion is a conceptual thing, it's also a business.' It seemed an obvious decision then for Frisoni to branch into fashion design, responding to the street-level sub-trends that often inspire fashion designers of reputable houses.

Working with a small team, Frisoni launched his own label for the freedom to express his ideas in design. Describing his work as cutting-edge, avant garde and of quality fabrication, the designer is often inspired by a particular piece of music, 'getting completely caught up in it and imagining the end product.' His Spring/Summer 2009/2010 collection was the first to introduce a women's line, catering to those customers who appreciate 'something special: a special fabric, special design, special button, special pocket.'
Most recently the designer developed a unique fabric made from bamboo, silk and wool, which falls and drapes in a similar way to a high quality jersey. At the time, he was unable to afford the rights to maintain the fabric, which were purchased by Giorgio Armani, but still uses the fabric in his work for his customers that want to 'feel delicious and look beautiful.'

Whether for men or women, Frisoni's clothes – often separates in neutral colour palettes – are of a directional shape and form, in that they may reflect a culture or costume not traditionally associated with the Western wardrobe.

1 Silk jacket and silk draped pants, A/W 10

His Spring/Summer 2009/2010 collection, for example, consisted of draped harem pants, deconstructed jackets and vests, and disproportionate shirting, which spoke of power and sensuality. Varying contours and unusual lines made for a visually enticing spectacle. Frisoni's work is deeply considered, with each collection aware of an overriding design philosophy and approach. His customer can therefore embrace such innovative styles with confidence, not hindered by tradition.

2 Wool bamboo shirt and
wool pants, A/W 10

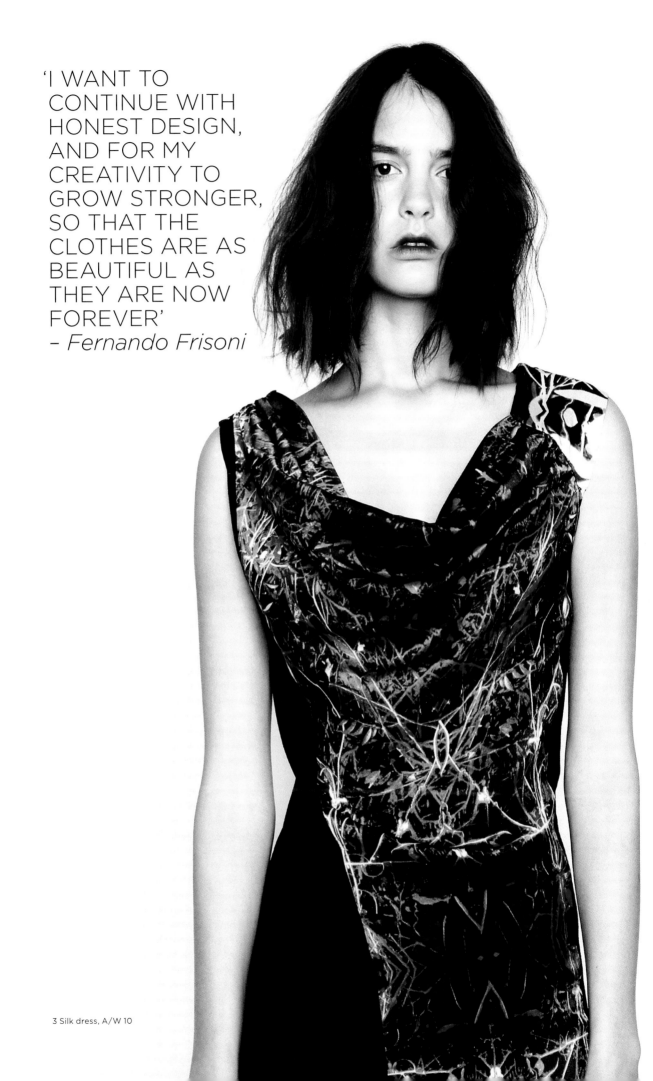

'I WANT TO
CONTINUE WITH
HONEST DESIGN,
AND FOR MY
CREATIVITY TO
GROW STRONGER,
SO THAT THE
CLOTHES ARE AS
BEAUTIFUL AS
THEY ARE NOW
FOREVER'
– *Fernando Frisoni*

3 Silk dress, A/W 10

FLAMINGO SANDS
JANE HAGES AND NICKY ROWSELL

When marketing manager Nicky Rowsell approached designer Jane
Hages with the idea to create a fashion business together, Hages was
apprehensive to say the least. 'If Nicky had asked me to create a t-shirt
and jeans label, I would have said no,' she explains. 'There were a lot of
fashion labels beginning at the time, but there wasn't many people
doing swimwear, and it really was a fresh idea.' And so Flamingo
Sands was born.

The designers are quick to establish that they are not a surf label,
but instead offer luxury swimwear that is fashion-driven and practical.
Established in 2004, the Melbourne-based duo won the Mercedes-Benz
Start-Up Program in the same year and showed their collection in a
New Generation parade at Australian Fashion Week in 2005. As Hages
explains, 'it was amazing for us to be recognised within a few months
of beginning; an affirmation that we were on the right path.' It was
indeed a signal of the future success of the label, which was picked up by
British department store Selfridges & Co. within the first six months.
'People started noticing us and saying "oh, you're stocked in Selfridges,
you must be good."'

While strongly reminiscent of Australian beach culture, Flamingo Sands is
at home in São Pãolo just as it is in Sydney, and is now stocked in over 100
stores around the world. The designers believe this popularity is partly
due to the strong marketing of their product. 'We definitely have a look
and try to build our brand each season with glamorous photo shoots,
an interactive website, distribution and editorial support.' Though like
any good fashion, it is the product that best markets itself.

1 Nylon and Lycra
bikini and cotton
singlet, S/S 09/10

While the swimwear is fashionable
in terms of trends, colours and
cuts, there is also something classic
about the various styles each
season. There seems a nostalgic
approach to each collection, as
if harking back to a glamorous
bygone era, be it with a one-piece
halter-neck or bandeau bikini.
The designers produce their
swimwear locally and spend
extensive time developing
innovative, original prints that are
inspired by vintage images, record
covers and video clips. Such prints

2 Nylon and Lycra one-piece
swimsuit and acid-washed
denim skirt, S/S 09/10

are used variously throughout each
collection, in different colourways
and styles, and carried through to
the complementing kaftans, beach
dresses, shorts and bags.

'WE'RE NOT A SURF BRAND. WE OFFER LUXURY SWIMWEAR THAT IS FASHION DRIVEN AND FUNCTIONAL' – Nicky Rowsell

3 Nylon and Lycra bikini, S/S 09/10

FLEUR WOOD
FLEUR WOOD

Each step in Fleur Wood's successful career has remained true to her core values and beliefs. Her luxurious collections of the same name – including clothing, homewares, and accessories – are ethically manufactured using no animal products, and a percentage of company profits are donated to charities in India, the greatest source of Wood's inspiration.

Beginning her own label in 1999, Wood had returned to Australia after living in the Indian Himalayas for two years where she worked on a cultural preservation project for the Tibetan exile government. At this time the business focused on product development, the importation of fabrics, shawls and various accessories from India, growing to include seasonal collections, beginning initially with four slips in several colourways. 'It has grown from a small intimates and homewares collection into a full lifestyle business,' explains Wood of the development. 'Our point of difference is that we're very much a lifestyle brand; it's not just about fashion, but also homewares and accessories.'

For Wood, inspiration comes from 'everywhere and everything', including film, books and photography. However it is her extensive travel that is the strongest influence on her work, which presents a paradox in itself: vintage detailing in modern silhouettes. And yet this is something Wood manages to produce in a resoundingly stylish manner. Sourcing fabrics and workmanship abroad, it is not rare to find ethnic prints finished with hand-stitched embroidery in her collections. 'I'm travelling a lot, and so I see different and unique things that I can put into the collections to keep the product fresh and exciting,' explains Wood. 'The resulting aesthetic is feminine in a way: we try to make clothes that make women feel good

1 Silk and satin dress, A/W 09

when they wear them.' Such an idea transcends the various lines of the Fleur Wood business, with an 'absolute synergy' between homewares and apparel, each 'building upon each other.'

In an industry that often sacrifices morality and quality for a bottom line, Wood is ardent on ensuring that the factories she works with are compliant with World Health Organisation standards, such as the payment of overtime wages, a satisfactory level of cleanliness and no child labour.

'It's just making sure all requirements are met,' she adds. 'We do try to help India as much as we can, as I think we have a responsibility to give back, and India has been a very good country to me.'

Wood's greatest pride is her network of four retail stores in Australia, which provide the designer with a way to 'communicate directly with the customer and really explain the product and concept.' She is keen on maintaining a high level of quality and expanding each range slowly and appropriately. 'I am really proud to be apart of the Australian fashion industry, and I believe we produce really amazing fashion given the resources available to us.'

2 Silk and satin top, Pakeha lace
vest and cotton drill pants, A/W 09

‘OUR POINT OF DIFFERENCE IS THAT
WE'RE VERY MUCH A LIFESTYLE BRAND'
– *Fleur Wood*

3 Habutai silk dress and
sequin jacket, A/W 09

FRIEDRICH GRAY
BEN POLLITT

Ben Pollitt is a designer of the rarest nature. He doesn't come from a fashion background, is not looking to take over the world, and you won't see a drop of champagne in his studio. Yet unlike the platform from which he works, his label Friedrich Gray is one of the greatest forces in upcoming fashion.

'I started helping a friend with some design,' tells Pollitt, 'and stumbled across the fact that it was possible to make a career out of it. I travelled to New York and people were commenting on the clothes I was wearing that I'd made myself. When I returned to Sydney there was no one I wanted to work for and so I started my own thing.' Pollitt's manner has remained humble and he has developed a business by building upon orders each season.

Friedrich Gray is best described as industrial androgyny. Pollitt designs for both men and women and uses high quality fabrics, such as leather and wool, to ensure the clothes last a lifetime. Inspired by music, art and historical references, he attempts to create pieces that aren't trend-specific or fashion statements, but that are solid, with a strong cut and can be worn every day. The idea of non-trend-specific clothing, that which is innately stylish, equals lifetime wearability. Perhaps the pinnacle of Pollitt's creative vision was presented in his Spring/Summer 2009/2010 collection on the eve of Australian Fashion Week. Aptly titled *Transgression,* the collection explored the limits of subversion, eroticism and counterculture, building upon his previous work and entering a new stylistic phase. While the clothes maintained the androgynous narrative of the Friedrich Gray label – stretched silhouettes, the binaries of textiles – there

1 Silk scarf and wool
dress, A/W 09

was also an exit from traditional colours, instead injecting saturated film colours and prints – green, yellow, orange and red – which were inspired by David Lynch's use of shadow and lighting in the film *Dune*.

Managing everything from design to production to marketing, Pollitt tells there are no plans to 'sell out', but instead continue making excellent product that is available to many. His current distribution includes stockists in Europe, the USA, and Australasia.

While his work speaks for itself, the young designer has had some help along the way, providing him with opportunities to expose his work on a broader level. In 2007 Pollitt won the Qantas Spirit of Youth Award (SOYA), which gave him 'incredible exposure and the opportunity to travel overseas,' with a cash prize of $5000, Qantas flights and mentorship from fashion icon Peter

2 Print from S/S 09/10 collection

Morrissey. 'It opens doors,' he tells. Pollitt also won the Designer Award, supported by Wool Innovation and presented by *Vogue* Australia. Pollitt was then selected by *Vogue* Australia editor Kirstie Clements as a protégé in the Australian Wool Innovation (AWI) project, which supported him in creating a collection using Australian merino wool and offered Pollitt the opportunity to visit factories in Asia to develop knitwear and fabric. He was sponsored to show this collection at Australian Fashion Week in 2008. As the designer explains, 'bringing this youthful energy into Woolmark has been a really good mix, and to have the editor of *Vogue* Australia supporting you is obviously great.'

In the few years he has been working as a designer, Pollitt has found his own way of designing. As he tells, 'I like that I don't come from the same angle as everyone else – it comes out in the product.'

3 Wool dress, S/S 09/10

4 Leather jacket and
denim jeans, A/W 09

'PEOPLE THINK
EVERYTHING
IS AMAZING
IN FASHION –
PARTIES AND
CHAMPAGNE
– BUT IT'S THE
COMPLETE
OPPOSITE,
AND IT'S BEEN A
STEEP LEARNING
CURVE FOR ME'
– *Ben Pollitt*

5 Leather jacket, silk singlet
and denim jeans, A/W 09

GAIL SORRONDA
GAIL REID

Gail Reid is something of an enigma in the design world. Not for her clothes, but because she leads a nomadic existence managing the Gail Sorronda label across two continents: in Paris she runs her business and designs her collections; and in Brisbane, where she grew up and studied design.

After completing a Bachelor of Fine Arts in Fashion Design from the Queensland University of Technology – 'which prepared me with some practical and technical skills that I needed to move forward in the industry,' explains Reid – the designer won the Mercedes-Benz Start-Up Award which provided her the opportunity to show her graduate collection *Angel At My Table* at Australian Fashion Week in 2005. 'From that,' tells Reid, 'I started my label and secured some stockists,' which allowed her to build upon the initial ideas presented in a broader, more commercially-oriented manner.

Heavily influenced by the built environment, evidenced by the use of contrasting forms, textures and structures in her clothing, Reid's inspiration is drawn from her emotional state at the time of designing. Reid's Spring/Summer 2009/2010 collection *Invasive Exotics* was inspired by her 2008 relocation to Paris where the designer worked closely with an Italian production company. This collection, Reid's seventh, drew upon her feeling of being lost and disconnected in a foreign environment and the subsequent awkward embrace. In a palette of black and white, Reid combined innumerable materials – from sheer white organza through to draped black silk – in a collection of dresses, skirts and tops that played on different eras: from high-necked Victorian pleated ruffles to scoop-necked flapper dresses, each adorned with varying combinations of feathers, frills and lace in an overwhelming melange of styles, just like Paris itself. And fittingly, Reid's intended aesthetic is that of 'opposite and equal reaction: monochromatic graphic silhouettes, abrupt in nature but feminine in feeling.'

As Reid explains of her changing locations, 'I'm rather nomadic, but the purpose remains the same; to continue building brand awareness and to open myself up to options of diversity and opportunity. I am developing this by exposing my creative identity to people that can help me extend myself as a designer. It's about constantly learning about technical and creative possibilities and understanding how different markets respond to what you do.' And, as Reid notes, she enjoys diversity and the idea of 'a global market that doesn't discriminate.'

1 Jersey top, silk georgette and tulle skirt, sequin and feather neckpiece and hairclip, S/S 09/10

Reid's eagerness to explore the creative and production process can be largely attributed to the capsule collection she was commissioned to create for Target Australia. 'Even though they gave me a very open brief, it made me focus on a commercial objective and process.' The large benefit of the Designers for Target concept was, obviously, the introduction of the brand to a much greater audience.

'MY INSPIRATION IS A
DIRECT RESPONSE TO
HOW I'M FEELING AT THE
TIME. MY DESIGNS ARE
AN APPROPRIATION OF
INSPIRED TRUTH'
– *Gail Reid*

2 Wool dress,
A/W 10

3 Silk organza
dress, A/W 10

While Paris-based, Reid has continued to show at Australian Fashion Week
'to communicate and celebrate a three-dimensional feeling and concept',
and maintains a wholesale network in Australia, which she manages
alongside her partner Atlas Harwood. The move, she tells, 'has opened
my eyes to an ever-growing, informed direction. The more I am exposed
to diversity, the more I realise what it is Gail Sorronda is about… where the
label is now and where I could dream it to be in the future. I am overcome
by different feelings all the time: fear, uncertainty, nervous energy; but I
am pushed by the overarching excitement of limitless possibility. Nothing
is or will ever be guaranteed but the journey is an adventure.'

4 Jersey and ostrich feather top, silk taffeta skirt and sequin and tulle neckpiece and mask. S/S 09/10

GARY BIGENI

GARY BIGENI

When Gary Bigeni showed his Spring/Summer collection at Australian Fashion Week in 2008, five years after his student show at the same event, he was overwhelmed by the feeling of achievement. 'The show was in the same room as it was when I was a student,' Bigeni recalls. 'Having all my teachers and family there supporting me, along with media and buyers... wow!' By this stage Bigeni's label was already big news in fashion circles, with his first collection being bought by Belinda Seper for the eponymous retail outlet The Corner Shop in Sydney's Paddington.

Bigeni studied fashion design at the TAFE Design Institute, graduating in 2002, before being selected to show his collection in a student show at Australian Fashion Week in 2003. The designer worked as a costume designer for children's group Hi-5 before being offered a job with fellow Australian Josh Goot, where he worked for a year before launching his own label. In doing so, Bigeni was able to exercise his skill and develop a stylistic direction before jumping in alone. He believes that 'it takes a while for a young designer to build a reputation, and media and buyers want a lot from you before they take you on. You need to stick at what you do and nail it.'

Judging by the designer's popularity, he can add 'nailed it' to his list of achievements. However, explains Bigeni, each day continues to be an uphill battle for younger designers. 'I'm financially supporting myself, and so I need to be careful about decisions I make,' noting that he would like to pick up some international stockists in the future. Menswear is also on the cards, though like his women's range, he would like to make it 'different to everything else out there.'

1 Silk and cotton
top, wool jacket
and spandex
leggings, A/W 09

The designer reacts to a feeling
or emotion when designing a
collection, rather than selecting a
specific theme. 'My Winter [2009]
collection was inspired by the
ocean, and so I twisted and draped
jersey – in a colour base of black,
ink and bottle green – in such a
way that reflected my idea.' Jersey
is a material often used by Bigeni,
with the intermittent addition of
leather, woven-base fabrics, wool
and silks, producing his clothes in
Australia. His clothing, which breaks
from traditional Australian fashion
style, challenges perceptions and
expectations of silhouettes, as he
attempts to create new shapes in
each collection. Bigeni's work is
not trend-specific, aiming to design
clothes that can be worn today or
in ten years' time. The intention is

2 Silk and cotton top and
spandex leggings, A/W 09

translated with simple and modern
dresses, skirts and tops that appear
effortless and elegant. 'It's about
creating a feeling for the wearer; I
want people to interpret my clothes
with their own style.'

3 Cotton dress, A/W 09

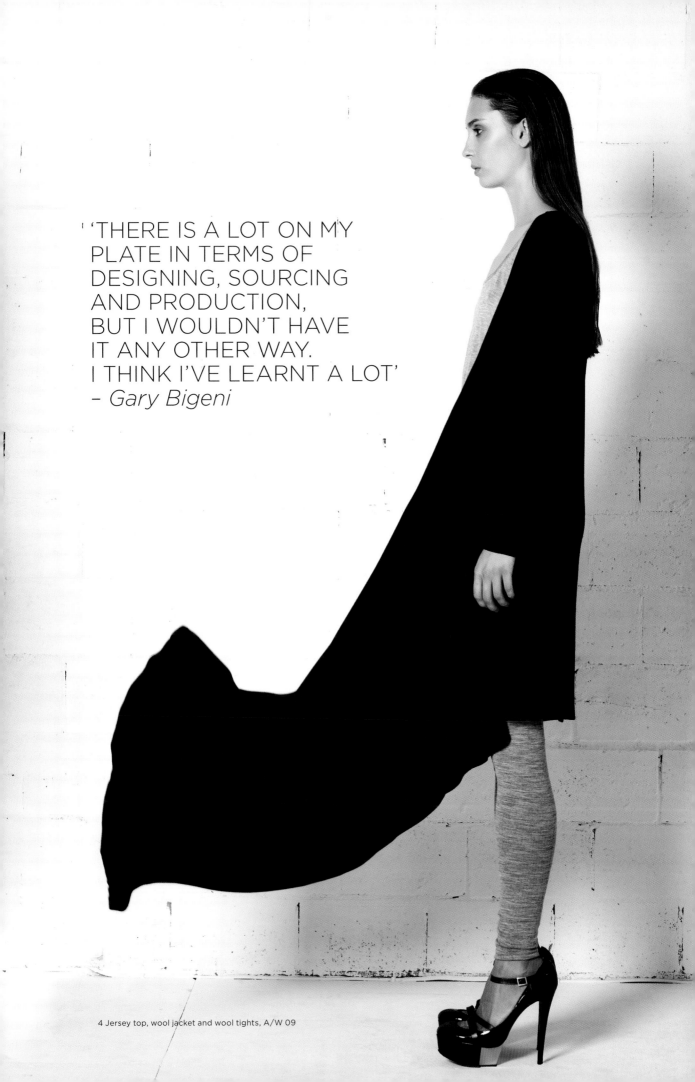

' 'THERE IS A LOT ON MY
PLATE IN TERMS OF
DESIGNING, SOURCING
AND PRODUCTION,
BUT I WOULDN'T HAVE
IT ANY OTHER WAY.
I THINK I'VE LEARNT A LOT'
– Gary Bigeni

4 Jersey top, wool jacket and wool tights, A/W 09

GINGER&SMART
ALEXANDRA AND GENEVIEVE SMART

The GINGER&SMART approach to fashion is perhaps best described
as 'quiet luxury'. Indeed, their work is of impeccable quality in its use
of materials and production, in harmony with their chic boutiques and
packaging. And yet the actual theme or style of the garments is as
understated as it is inspiring. From candles and body products, through to
luggage and apparel, GINGER&SMART is the epitome of design that is at
once intelligent, beautiful and relevant.

Sisters Alexandra and Genevieve Smart bring to the label varying creative
energies and business experience. Prior to creating the label in 2002,
Alexandra worked as a fashion editor and publisher, and Genevieve as
a designer for the likes of Lisa Ho and Zimmermann. Their close familial
relationship and strict design philosophies create a business that is
admired and respected on numerous levels.

GINGER&SMART started small, entering the market with a collection
of scented candles and leather accessories with a view to creating
a greater lifestyle brand that incorporated fashion as its figurehead.
Launching firstly with Browns Focus in London, it wasn't long before
the GINGER&SMART label became an icon of Australian fashion design,
winning its designers several awards in their first few years. As they tell
of such attention, 'it was like being thrown into the spotlight slightly
undressed. We had overwhelming support from local suppliers, media and
buyers. The door is always open to fresh ideas and a new perspective.'

Juggling the various product categories and aspects of their business,
both Genevieve and Alexandra are intent on maintaining a consistent

1 Silk and chiffon top and acetate rayon pants, S/S 09/10

2 Washed silk habouti dress, S/S 09/10

message throughout, which is a defining element of GINGER&SMART. When inspiration finds them – 'usually most inconveniently' – the pair work together to create meaning and clarity in their ideas. They describe their work as 'effortless modern chic', although the clothes have a more potent individual flavour than that of competing fashion labels, one that promotes the wearer in a strong light. Reminiscent of a jungle, with lightweight safari suits, gladiator sandals and bold wooden jewellery, or of kites, with sheer, billowing pants and shifts, each collection presents a strong vision of women. Perhaps it's the personal style of the designers, for they both forged successful careers at a young age, or maybe it is their innate belief in the strength of women as characters in the story that is life. The pair believe their customer 'can be any age – it's an attitude. She is comfortable in her own skin.' Either way, the GINGER&SMART aesthetic is highly individual and therefore recognisable in the market, and strongly contributes to the diversity of Australian fashion.

3 Cotton and cashmere
dress and wool blend
jacket, A/W 09

4 Washed silk
habouti dress,
A/W 09

Working most often with texture and prints, the designers classically
drape on mannequins when creating each collection. The Smart sisters
prefer to work on a mannequin as opposed to sketching in an attempt
to create a product that resonates with people and their bodies, and
so feel it best to work in three dimensions. Leathers form a strong part
of each collection, with the business having grown from accessories,
and GINGER&SMART age and wash these before use to give them a
suppleness and individuality. 'We devote a lot of time in developing
the perfect colour in fabric, leather or fragrance. We experiment with
new techniques working with new technology.' The pair have most
recently developed a new thread that charges with daylight and glows
translucently in the evening. Such experiments are part of the future of
GINGER&SMART, as they 'hope to keep it interesting and venture into new
areas that inspire us.'

'THE DOOR IS
ALWAYS OPEN
TO FRESH IDEAS
AND A NEW
PERSPECTIVE'
– *Alexandra Smart*

5 Cotton and nylon
trench coat, A/W 06

6 Silk cotton voile dress,
S/S 09/10

7 Triacetate jacket and
viscose dress, S/S 09/10

GORMAN
LISA GORMAN

An environmentally-friendly label, the high quality clothes of designer Lisa Gorman are made from certified-organic fibres and produced using conventional farming methods. The ethos of environmental consciousness stems further than garment production. Gorman styles are typically not season-specific, but instead function as timeless additions to a wardrobe, avoiding contribution to fashion landfill after merely a few months. While organic clothing was emerging in Australia, Gorman was the first label to introduce the concept to the world of stylish, runway fashion.

Landing her first fashion job in 1998 for bridal designer Mariana Hardwick, first in retail and merchandising and later in design, Lisa Gorman unintentionally began her own label by producing a one-off, exhibition-style collection for Melbourne store Fat4. Selling out instantly, Gorman was approached by other retailers and so began producing collections on a seasonal basis. Perplexed by the lack of sustainable clothing despite textiles on the market that lent themselves to the concept, the environment was on Gorman's agenda from the beginning. 'I was interested in why people didn't do it,' explains Gorman. 'I do it because of the effect the fashion industry has on the planet. I felt that from a fashion perspective there wasn't much happening on the green front – not many brands do it well or at all, and smaller brands don't have the resources.'

Having launched a second line in 2007, Gorman Organic, consisting of basics and underwear, designer Lisa Gorman and her team have sought to not only become carbon neutral, but also to help reverse the effects of fashion on the environment through both their own product and as a flag-bearer for the growing green fashion industry. Gorman have looked

not only at the
emissions of
their own office
and stores,
but also of
the factories
that produce

1 Silk dress and cotton
pants S/S 08/09

their clothing, the shopping bags
and garment tags, and even the
stationery they use daily. In fact,
Gorman choose to only work with
suppliers with proven, credible
environmental policies, which has
seen several companies rethink the
way they do business.

As Lisa Gorman explains, they have
researched 'right down the line.'
Gorman has managed to reduce
the use of garment packaging by
an astounding 90%, and what they
do use is recyclable. It isn't just
a marketing ploy that drives the
designer and her team to strive for
sustainability. 'If you're going to be
involved,' says Gorman, 'it has to
be for the long haul. A marketing

ploy is detrimental to your business.
There is so much of it going on, and
you need to have the customer's
trust.' It is this trust that has seen
the Gorman label grow so rapidly,
built through initiatives outside the
doors of the store.

With the assistance of an in-house
environmental consultant, Gorman
has developed innovative organic
fabrics, such as an Australian
organic wool product which is
produced in conjunction with The
Merino Company. 'Supply goes up
and down in the world,' explains the
designer. 'Generally we get [organic
cotton] from Turkey or India, and
we produce most of the clothing
in Asia, close to the source, to

2 Gorman 'Ship Shop', Melbourne

avoid excessive shipping.' Gorman further explains that Australia is not in a position to be growing vast amounts of organic cotton due to our limited manufacturing capabilities; however 50% of Gorman's product is produced onshore. Materials such as bamboo are also used in threads that require more drape or a different finish, and are grown naturally while requiring much less water than other garment fibres. Organic textiles can be costly and affect the price of a garment for a customer. Gorman chooses not to compete with the mass, low-budget market, instead aligning her business with the middle market that is more willing to invest in quality pieces.
'If a customer can wear it and wash it over and over again, then it's good value.'

In 2008, the brand launched an organic Ship Shop at Australian Fashion Week as a consumer-driven campaign highlighting sustainable clothing and retailing. Essentially a shipping container, the store is fully transportable and contains no carry bags and no cash register. Inside, however, are change rooms and the full range of Gorman clothing, which the customer is welcomed to try on and have the product sent to their home via the online store.

Gorman believes that each action, no matter how small, contributes to environmental sustainability. 'They [the fashion industry] see it as more of a battle rather than something they want to jump into and go for. It's a long term thing and fashion moves so fast. It takes time to invest in the partners you want to work with on sustainable collections.' This restriction, she hopes, will be lessened with textile mills more readily supplying organic materials with growth in consumer demand.

'I FELT THAT FROM A FASHION PERSPECTIVE THERE WASN'T MUCH HAPPENING ON THE GREEN FRONT – NOT MANY BRANDS DO IT WELL OR AT ALL AND SMALLER BRANDS DON'T HAVE THE RESOURCES'
– *Lisa Gorman*

3 Silk skirt and tie, wool t-shirt and leather bag, A/W 07

HOTEL BONDI SWIM
DAMION FULLER AND FERN LEVACK

Australia's geographic relationship with the ocean creates a unique and unrivalled beach culture. It makes sense, then, that Australia has often led swimwear design internationally, continually creating new styles that react to trends, the climate, and the needs of their wearer. And just as Australian designers don't create heavy winter collections, the swimwear crown remains firmly Australian. Hotel Bondi Swim, named after the radiant beach culture of Bondi, is part of this iconic group of swimwear designers, and just like its namesake, radiates with fresh ideas.

The designers, couple Damion Fuller and Fern Levack, both bring varied and extensive experience to the label. Such experience has given their work and business manner a polished professionalism from the beginning, launching their label with a runway collection at Australian Fashion Week in 2008. As well as a fashion launch, Hotel Bondi Swim produced a book with photographer Derek Henderson of inspirational images of the unknown, and perhaps more beautiful, side of Bondi: 'backstreet wholefood stores, the crumbling peach and cream façade of the Bondi Hotel, the colourful fish at North Bondi's boat ramp.' The book paid homage to the underlying inspiration of the label and captured the essence of what it represents. It is projects such as this that distinguish Hotel Bondi Swim from many other swimwear labels as they aim to connect with their customers, admirers and locals.

Fuller, trained in industrial design, worked for the inimitable Australian brand Mambo as an accessories and menswear designer for several years, as well as consulting several other brands including Marcs, Puma and Rip Curl. Levack, trained in fashion and textile design, worked with

1 Lycra one-piece
swimsuit, S/S 08/09

2 Lycra bikini,
S/S 08/09

Collette Dinnigan ('I spent nearly four years under her tutelage and learnt invaluable lessons about business, sales and the design process') before creating her own label Kitten as part of her final year university project, which was soon after stocked and supported by General Pants Co. as well as Harvey Nichols, Selfridges and David Jones. It was with Kitten, during its eight-year lifespan, that Fuller and Levack began their strong working relationship that was to see the birth of Hotel Bondi Swim as an evolution of their joint creative vision. As Fuller tells, 'I was always more interested in the process of bringing an idea from concept to reality.' This progressive notion, combined with Levack's love of textile printing and illustration, has only strengthened their relationship.

Levack explains that the style of Hotel Bondi Swim combines 'the functionality of vintage fits, such as balconette bras and ruched one-pieces, with laidback and colourfully Australian prints in watercolour illustrations and paper cut-outs. Our styles are simple and unpretentious whilst maintaining an element of luxury [with] high-quality trims and production techniques.' Prints, often created with watercolour and gouache, maintain all of the 'flaws and subtleties' of the original artwork. 'Each season there are some special prints in the range that reflect our strong environmental and cultural slant,' explain the pair, noting a print with miniature Jane Austen-style portraits featuring the faces and names of the Bondi Boardriders' Club, and more recently, a mint green print that pays homage to Bob Brown, the leader of the Australian Greens political party. It is this relaxed and often humorous approach to swimwear that attracts customers from every corner of the globe.

'OUR INSPIRATION IS OUR BACKYARD,
BONDI BEACH – THE LOCAL
IDENTITIES, LANDMARKS AND LEGENDS'
– *Fern Levack*

3 Lycra bikini, S/S 08/09

J'ATON COUTURE
JACOB LUPPINO AND ANTHONY PITTORINO

J'Aton Couture is the fusion of designers Jacob Luppino and Anthony Pittorino. Following a number of years working for various design houses in Melbourne, their dynamic partnership began in 1995 when they embarked upon a shared journey to push the boundaries of contemporary couture. In 2010 the two designers relocated their growing business to New York which, as they tell, was inevitable as they chase their market. 'We're not moving to become superstars; we just can't work naturally [in Australia] as our product is still a bit over-the-top for the Australian lifestyle. Women don't wear a couture gown to the ballet or opera in Australia, and so we need to find our clients.'

Luppino and Pittorino met while studying at the Melbourne College of Textiles, which they found to be 'a really basic course about patternmaking and construction rather than creative design.' For the first of the three years of study the two designers disliked each other and were intensely competitive. Upon graduation Luppino began creating clothing for private clients from his home, while Pittorino worked for various bridal studios. 'We became mates after finishing,' explains Pittorino, 'and then five years after graduating Jacob suggested we begin our own business, which was a daunting prospect at 23 years old.' With $5000 between them, the designers rented a shop and placed their first advertisement in *Vogue* Australia. 'No one in Australia knew what couture was, let alone how to spell it. We were doing outlandish outfits for weddings, engagements, birthdays and bar mitzvahs when celebrities began catching on and we started dressing some Australian television stars.' It is this support that has driven J'Aton Couture, according to the designers. 'Without Australian celebrities we wouldn't have any respect or credibility in this country.'

1 Silk and metal corseted top and skirt, A/W 08

The journey has not been easy for Luppino and Pittorino. The majority of J'Aton Couture clients are based overseas and have been introduced to the label by word-of-mouth. The pair has never had financial backing to assist in growing their business but have found potential investors in New York. As they explain, 'we have been approached by a lot of people, but no-one has understood how much is behind a great brand. People think a million dollars is a lot in Australia, but it is nothing for a fashion house – it won't even get you a year of advertising in US *Vogue*.' Moving overseas to relaunch their business is a bold move, but the designers are confident with the decision. 'When you are the one steering the ship you know you have to put in the days and nights to make it happen.'

New York has been chosen as J'Aton Couture's new base as there is strong a demand for couture product. The designers explain that while people in Australia like their work, they have trouble selling it because of the price point. 'It's inevitable that a dress will be more than $3000 as it might have been constructed from French lace and silks and taken tens of hours to construct. On a world scale, people are shocked by how cheap our product is, but in Australia people think we're ripping them off.' While the label may be based outside Australia for a time, Luppino and Pittorino confirm that they do intend to open a boutique at home after they have re-established their business.

The designers have taught themselves the art of haute couture. While their fashion course focused on patterns and construction, there was no instruction in draping or creating darts or engineering. 'We had to experiment with our mannequins,' explains Pittorino fittingly, with scraps and off-cuts of calico lining the floors and benches of the design studio. Their work today uses a lot of boning and corsetry, drawing on their infinite knowledge of how to engineer a bodice on a 'real woman'. With luxurious fabrics the designers use draping to create an individual silhouette without the use of a pattern because 'it wouldn't fit the next person as it's created for each client. It's all about individuality and personal needs.'

While fashion is a tough industry, particularly so for couture artists, Luppino and Pittorino are very grateful for the experiences they have had. 'You have to enjoy the journey even though it's hard. We've created something out of nothing and love every day. We don't dwell on the negative but appreciate the amazing experiences we have had. We love fashion and being involved with it.'

2 Silk and wool mesh body suit
embroidered with fine silk gauze
and cotton muslin, A/W 05

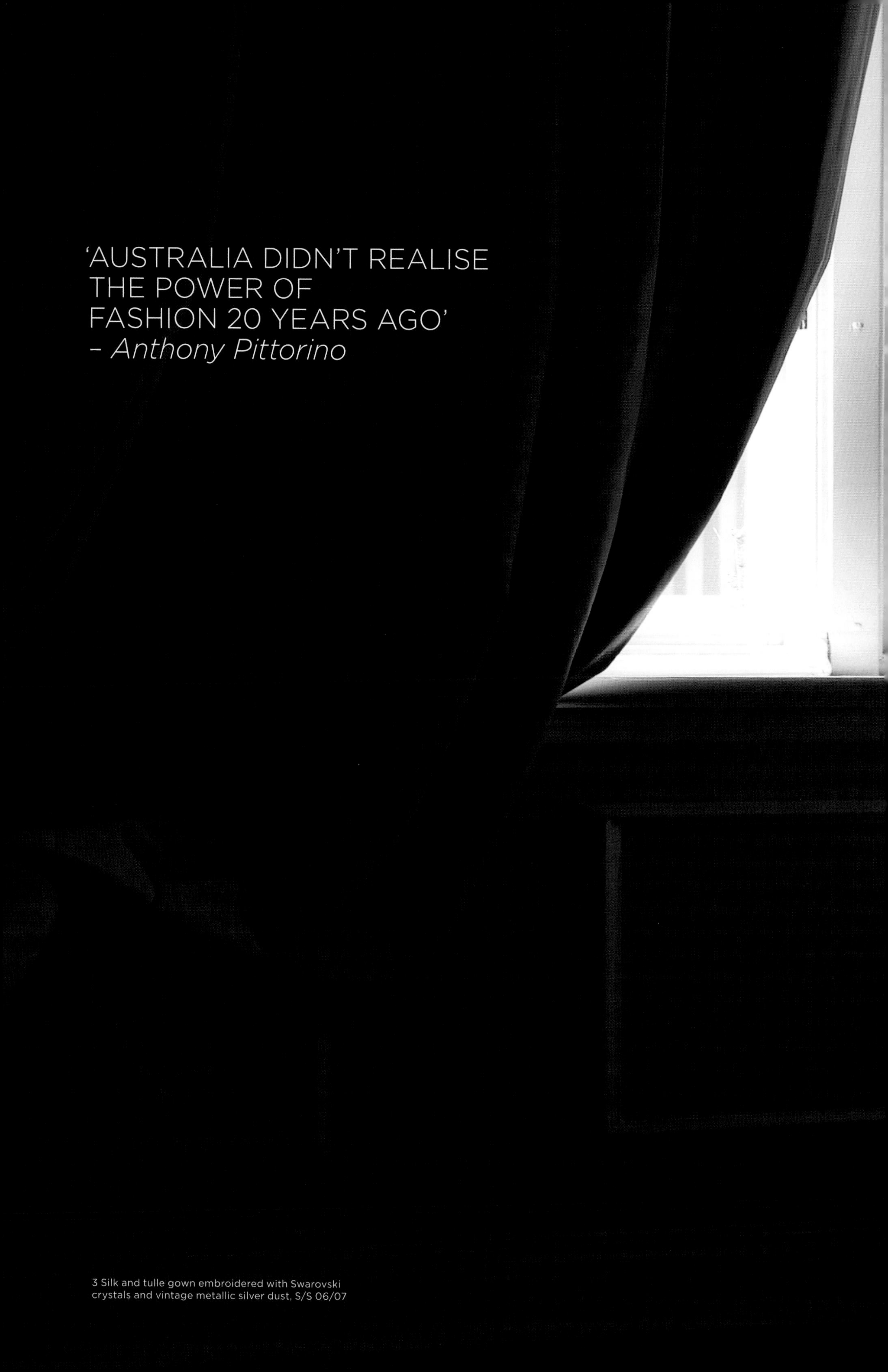

'AUSTRALIA DIDN'T REALISE
THE POWER OF
FASHION 20 YEARS AGO'
– *Anthony Pittorino*

3 Silk and tulle gown embroidered with Swarovski
crystals and vintage metallic silver dust, S/S 06/07

JAYSON BRUNSDON
JAYSON BRUNSDON

Eager to get started in the fashion industry, Jayson Brunsdon left the fashion course he was studying at the University of Sydney after two years and began making clothes to sell at Paddington Markets. A chance job as an illustrator for fashion magazines led Brunsdon to work as a stylist and editor in New York and London before returning to Australia to work for the then wildly popular Morrissey Edmiston label in the early 1990s.

As Brunsdon tells, 'it was great fun working with Morrissey Edmiston. They were at their peak and it was crazy; we had celebrities visiting the showroom all the time and they'd just sold to New York and were to later open the first Australian Fashion Week [in 1996].' While Brunsdon felt that he gained a lot by working with two of Australia's most prominent designers, it was time to move on, and after working with Peter Morrissey for nine years following the Morrissey-Edmiston split, Brunsdon left his position as creative director to focus on launching his own label.
'I wanted to express something of what women wanted, and also express myself creatively.'

Breaking into the industry alone was made easier for Brunsdon, having already worked with media and buyers for many years. Though like any business, starting out was tough. 'While the initial years were successful, they were also extremely stressful; there were seven-day weeks and no cash flow.' Working alongside his partner Aaron Elias, who manages the business, the designer has successfully shown his collections in New York, maintains strong international distribution and has opened three retail stores. He finds that Australasia is his prime retail market, which led to the opening of his Singapore store in 2007 after his first in Sydney's Strand

1 Wool and silk satin dress, A/W 07

Arcade in 2005. His third and fourth stores opened in Bondi Junction and Chapel St, Melbourne in 2009. As Brunsdon tells, 'I love showing throughout Asia as they are very responsive to Australian design and an individual retail environment is ideal because you can really control your image.'

Brunsdon's background as an illustrator is evident in his designs. Cocktail dresses, evening gowns and soft suiting have a sense of whimsy and are elegantly constructed from fine silks and luxurious materials. 'I draw my inspiration from women – how they want to feel and look – as well as visual imagery.' The glamour of Brunsdon's work is often reminiscent of the Golden Age of Hollywood – a period heavily influenced by the freehand narrative of illustration while photography was finding its feet. Jayson Brunsdon has most recently introduced a range of daywear, which is 'affordable and can take you from day to cocktail party.' Complementing the range is a collection of vintage-inspired jewellery as well as leather bags, belts and shoes. 'When you're styling a show you want the whole thing to come together the way you see it in your mind. It is a natural progression for us to develop accessories, and we're very excited about it.'

2 Silk satin and sequin dress, A/W 07

Brunsdon's artistic mastery has earned him a place as one of Australia's most prominent and well-respected fashion designers, and led him to feature as a judge on the reality television program *Project Runway Australia* in 2008. 'I was reluctant at first,' explains the designer. 'But the talent was great and it was a lot of fun. We keep producing creative people here in Australia, and in the last 10 years the world has noticed, first with cinema and art, and now with fashion.'

3 Silk taffeta and
sequin dress, A/W 07

4 Wool dress, A/W 07

'I THINK YOU'RE ALWAYS LIVING IN THE
FUTURE IN THIS BUSINESS, ALWAYS THINKING
THE NEXT YEAR WILL BE BETTER, WHICH
DRIVES YOU TO CONTINUE'
– Jayson Brunsdon

5 Wool and silk dress, A/W 07

JIMMY D
JAMES DOBSON

Restrained and unassuming, New Zealand label Jimmy D came about naturally for designer James Dobson. With the discovery of fashion magazines while in high school, particularly titles like *i-D, The Face* and *Pavement,* Dobson found fashion photography he could relate to. 'There was a blurring of the lines between fashion and art, and often in quite a raw, unpolished way,' he tells. 'Growing up in the suburbs, this was the first time fashion seemed accessible to me.'

Later completing a degree in photography, Dobson turned his hand to patternmaking and worked part-time in fashion retail while he found his feet and ideas formed. 'All the while I was jotting down ideas for collections and clothes,' he explains almost secretly. 'It wasn't until I returned from a year in London that I felt my ideas were good enough to make a reality.' And so Jimmy D was born, albeit quietly. Dobson showed his sketches and samples to the owners of the Wellington store he was working in, who happened to like the product and immediately placed orders. Spurring the development of a full collection, the designer was then selected to show in a new generation collection at Australian Fashion Week, winning the Mercedes-Benz Start-Up award in 2005. 'It was amazing exposure, and the business has grown steadily ever since.'

'I'll often be walking down the street and see the way a dress gets caught by the wind, and for a second it looks like something completely different. Maybe it's just that I need glasses, but it can be quite inspiring.' Using references like this, with the more thematic influences of film, photography and literature, Dobson builds his collections with 'faith that it will all come together and make sense in the end.' His seemingly effortless clothes can be categorised as having a New Zealand aesthetic – with a darker colour palette and sense of humour – but the designer believes it is not a conscious inspiration, but something 'too ingrained to know to what extent it comes from an internal or external place.' Indeed, Dobson's use of contrast, be it masculine versus feminine or sporty versus luxury, adds a constant push and pull in his work that ensures it doesn't become too serious. 'I like to make sure there is some kind of quirky print or a design feature that throws it just a little. I like fashion when it doesn't take itself too seriously.' Without a strictly conscious design mind, Dobson has allowed himself to turn his creative pursuits into a viable business that keeps him inspired 'year after year.'

His work, which is produced in New Zealand, is often distinguished by a particular and often voluminous use of fabric: 'there is nothing I like

1 Silk georgette oversized t-shirt, printed cotton t-shirt (worn underneath) and marle leggings, S/S 06/07

more than seeing a woman glide around with sheer layers of fabric enveloping her.' Balancing such volume with contoured pieces, such as panelled sci-fi inspired slips and leggings, Dobson works with silk georgette and organza, creating a luxury base upon which he dabbles with the contrast of 'sporty t-shirting fabrics or tech-y high shine polyesters and sequins.' An interesting mix, Dobson has found a niche in the market and is in regular contact with his customers,

'THE STARTING POINTS FOR MY COLLECTIONS ARE BECOMING MORE AMBIGUOUS, BUT THERE IS ALWAYS A FOCUS AND CLARITY THAT COMES TO THE PROCESS AS I WORK THROUGH IT'
– James Dobson

2 Lacquered polyester mesh top and elastic corset (worn underneath), A/W 09

working still in the stores that stock his clothing. 'The Jimmy D customer can be anyone from the fashion savvy twentysomethings to women in their fifties,' he believes. 'The thing that I think unites them is confidence, fearlessness and independence.'

Managing his business as well as designing collections, Dobson has his hands full, yet seems to thrive on his creative visions, which have led him most recently to open a store in Auckland. Children of Vision stocks Dobson's own label, as well as imports such as Bernhard Willhelm, Rad Hourani and Postweiler Hauber. As he tells, 'I like showing my collection alongside other designers – the reality is that very few people wear one label from head to toe, so it makes sense to show in a context that reflects this.' His ideal plan for the store is to see it grow alongside Jimmy D, creating a lifestyle that allows Dobson to travel the world buying for the store whilst simultaneously selling his label. If there ever was a one-man show, Dobson is it. He balances his achievements coyly, simply suggesting that he is a creative person but knows that the business side of things is just as important.

3 Wool skirt, viscose polo-neck top, silk georgette vest and cotton voile scarf, A/W 07

JONATHAN WARD
DESIGN AND COUTURE
and R.M.WILLIAMS
JONATHAN WARD

Born and raised on a remote farm, Jonathan Ward began his career in the design world on the cusp of Australia's fashion revolution to become one of the country's only, and best-regarded, haute couture artists. Having seen many changes in the local industry, and with unparalleled technical knowledge, Ward remains an eminent figure of Australian fashion.

'Couture is not as rare now as it was when I began at least 20 years ago,' says Ward. 'However, there is a big difference between a cut-and-sew and actually doing a proper consultancy with a client: looking at their figure, their colouring; finding fabrics; sketching; making toiles in calico to ensure it is cut well on the body. And the reason that it's probably still somewhat a niche industry is that it's not a big money-making area. It is extremely time-consuming.' And, indeed, Ward too experienced this contradiction throughout his career: of enjoying and wanting to create one-off, specially commissioned pieces, but having difficulty finding the time and specialty assistance for such work.

Bridalwear is a market that bridges the gap between couture dedication and price accessibility. 'I did bridal because it helped pay the bills,' says Ward, 'but also because it is very individual, and at that stage, very few people were doing beautiful, lean, simple silhouettes for brides. It was all the big balloon skirts, puff skirts, big, big, big! I just saw bridal as being quite chic, understated and elegant. Australia is very different to the rest of the world in that there is not a lot of places to wear things more than once or twice, unless it's a very classic black dress, and so bridalwear fills the gap.' And with Ward's established couture profile, he was able to attract customers that knew and respected the elegance of his work. 'Most of the brides that came to me were a bit more mature, and so they had that sophisticated sense of style.' With his bridal work – and, in fact, all couture work – Ward insisted on emphasising the concept of corsetry inside a gown or dress to give a woman more form and fit. 'I have a true belief that the inside of the garment is as important as the outside. It's a bit like architecture, building something that's going to work with a woman's figure. There are things like design, line and direction, colour, proportion and fit, to consider.'

After working for several years with Robert Burton, Ward relocated to New York ('which didn't last long, but was great experience'), before returning to Australia. 'There wasn't a lot happening in Australian fashion at the time,' he recalls. 'A brand like RM [Williams] was quite hip. Outside of that there were big brands like Carla [Zampatti] and Trent Nathan.' Ward slowly began creating one-off pieces for personal clients at home, which 'quickly transcended into making things for Belinda Green for Miss World and for young, unknown model Elle McPherson. Everything just snowballed as I took on word-of-mouth clients and it became my full-time business.' While Ward's couture business now sits on the side of his full-time role as creative director of R.M. Williams, he believes that although it is expensive and time-consuming, the couture customer is out there and always will be. 'I think a lot of people don't really understand that no one is perfectly proportioned and you can only alter garments so much, so couture has a relevant place in fashion design. It's a very

1 Hand-dyed silk taffeta gown with ostrich feathers and crystal detailing, 2009

old craft, and although Australia is quite a young country, a lot of younger designers understand and are utilising tailoring and couture techniques and giving them a modern edge. For a long time there was a move away from classic tailoring – when everything was very big, loose and easy – but to a certain degree that look of very nipped and tight is back in those body-conscious fabrics of velvets and silks. Tailoring has had a big resurgence.'

When working with a client, Ward believes the end result is a compromise between the client's brief and requirements and his own sense of style. 'I like things that have a balance of fabrics and textures,' he tells. 'And perhaps it's my upbringing, growing up with one brand [R.M. Williams], but I think it's about keeping the styling classic but giving things a modern twist with colour or accessories. I also use natural fibres, because I think they drape incredibly well. But definitely, I've always considered accessories a very important part of an entire look, and often with commissions it's about a head-to-toe look, so [we consider] what sort of earring the woman is going to wear, what bag she is going to carry. It's great to see that accessories have come to the forefront of fashion, because they really are important.'

Ward's position as executive designer of R.M. Williams, which began in 2001, has allowed him to make the brand appeal to a broader market and to expand its women's range, both of which provided him with a challenge that he desired. 'I thought long and hard about the job offer, but I'd nearly dressed everybody and you get to stage where you either expand in a much bigger way or you begin to stale.' At this stage in Ward's career, he was also selling a ready-to-wear collection by the name of Jonathan Ward Salon to David Jones, which he ceased to allow him the time to focus on his new role. 'R.M. is such an iconic Australian brand, and I'd always worn it growing up. I thought it would be so nice to take this brand to the world and to be the first designer to come on board [since R.M. Williams] and have the chance to reinvent it... to take the history of the brand and do something special without losing the integrity of it. To give it a new lease of life.'

In many ways, Ward's placement at R.M. Williams is akin to the placement of Christopher Bailey at Burberry, charged with reinventing a national yet staid icon for a modern audience. And just as Bailey was successful, so to has Ward been. Womenswear, first and foremost, has been considerably developed with much more depth, including the addition of accessories and footwear, as well as a new childrenswear line. And yet, for Ward, the most educational and interesting part of his work has been working with the craftspeople at R.M. Williams' South Australian factory. 'They have been making boots and cutting things by hand, and maybe it's my background that my roots took me back there, but I don't think there is another Australian brand with such a legacy as R.M. Williams.' Nor, either, is there such a brand with a bespoke concept built around footwear and leather, and one that has not only maintained its reputation domestically, but also built a following internationally.

Ward hasn't moved the brand too quickly as he tells, 'a brand is only as good as the customer that supports it. A brand will die if it's not reinvented to suit a younger market, but that doesn't mean you can walk away from the market that supports it. What we have done is make it more of a lifestyle brand.'

'A BRAND IS ONLY
A GOOD AS THE
CUSTOMER THAT
SUPPORTS IT'
– *Jonathan Ward*

2 Linen oilskin jacket, moleskin jodhpurs, and
leather boots with hand-plaited kangaroo leather
straps, collaboration with Catherine Martin, A/W 08

JOSH GOOT

JOSH GOOT

When Josh Goot was studying Media, Art & Production at the University of Technology, Sydney, he began making graphic-printed t-shirts as a side project. Interested in communication, fashion design became an outlet for the creative artist to express himself, and in 2004 his cult label was born. Beginning as unisex wardrobe essentials crafted from cotton jersey, the business has grown with the designer, seeing him win the Tiffany & Co. Young Designer Award in 2005 and score a *Women's Wear Daily* cover in the same year.

Goot, untrained in fashion design and production, has found the process of building a label a great challenge, though enjoys the trial-and-error nature of creating. 'I was predominantly interested in media and communications,' explains the designer, 'and I have tried to bring fashion into that realm, because that's how I consider it – a form of communication through the shape, fabric, colour and detail.' It's an interesting idea, and one that bodes well with the cool aesthetic of the designer's work, which finds inspiration in abstract references. 'We take these abstract points and embark on building a collection through interpretation and really opening up our minds,' he adds. With a new print story each season and clever use of draping and wrapping in figure-hugging, fluid fabrics, Goot also allows his customer to interpret the clothing and bring to it their own personality.

The Tiffany & Co. Designer of the Year Award proved 'a big help' in building momentum and gaining attention for the emerging label: 'that was a great moment for us,' says Goot. The attention led to a partnership with the Australian Wool Innovation (AWI), with whom Goot collaborated in the area of textile technology to develop unique fabrics.

2 Viscose
elastane dress,
S/S 07/08

1 Viscose jacket,
viscose tank
and nylon
elastane
leggings,
S/S 07/08

Soon after, Goot was selected to create a capsule collection for mega-retailer Target. This line was received with varied criticism in relation to the idea of 'fast fashion': many of the pieces bore a resemblance to the style of Goot's main line, comparatively much more expensive. This difference has been questioned of other similar chain-store collaborations, but as Goot explains, 'It was a way for us to take Australian wool to a greater audience, and a nice gift to give back [to AWI], as well as a financial gift to ourselves, as it's really hard trying to build an independently owned and run fashion label in Australia, or anywhere in the world. It's an expensive business, and I've been blessed that such opportunities have come my way.'

Goot is strongly involved with running his label in both a creative and directorial capacity. 'I've realised it is something I have to be involved in and that there is a great synergy between finance and creativity. It takes a while to see, but they can coexist really well.' This hands-on approach to his

3 Silk viscose dress,
S/S 09 (northern
hemisphere)

4 Silk viscose tank,
shell and skirt, S/S 09
(northern hemisphere)

business has seen Goot move his runway collections from New York to London Fashion Week, explaining simply that the clothes had changed. 'When we went to New York we were in the process of self-discovery; we had always believed in an aesthetic which has been consistent from then to now, but a lot of other things relating to the brand grew up a lot and became less relevant to the American market. Magazines and shops were calling us in Europe, so we looked at this information and decided we should try it.' In late 2009, Goot opened his first retail store in Sydney's Paddington, on the cusp of his exaggerated graphic-printed clothing reaching fever pitch attention.

Showing in London as opposed to the overcrowded schedule in New York has allowed Goot to be recognised for his clean, modern work, earning him a position as finalist in the prestigious el Botón-MANGO Fashion Awards. Sponsored by Spanish fast-fashion group MANGO, Goot was nominated alongside Richard Nicoll and Jean Pierre Braganza for the prize of $EU300, 000, for which he submitted several pieces. 'It's a vote of confidence,' claims the designer. 'Sometimes you get so into your own work it is hard to subjectively assess what you're doing.'

5 Cotton hooded
dress, S/S 07/08

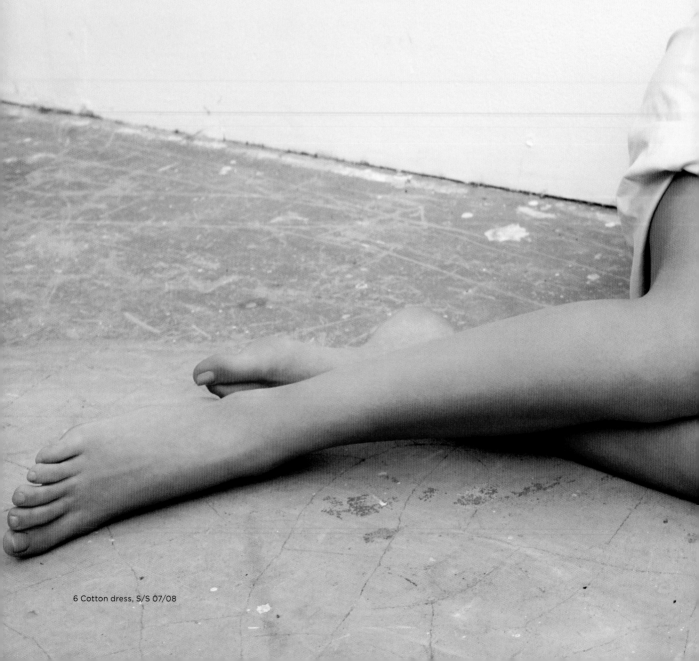

'I AM INTERESTED IN CAPTURING A
POINT OF VIEW AND COMMUNICATING
IT THROUGH FASHION'
– *Josh Goot*

6 Cotton dress, S/S 07/08

KAREN WALKER
KAREN WALKER

When Karen Walker opened the style.com website at 5am the day after her first New York Fashion Week show in 2006, she was nervous to say the least. 'I was hiding my head under the pillow,' tells Walker jokingly. As the screen loaded with images from her collection, the designer was overwhelmed by a heading that read 'NYC WELCOMES KAREN WALKER'. The success of this internationally renowned designer is a far cry from her chance beginning in 1989 when, armed with only $100 she bought fabric to make some shirts that were bought by the boutique she was working in.

Walker trained in fashion design at a small school in Auckland before launching her own label. 'I can't remember ever wanting to do anything else from an early age,' explains Walker. 'When I was five years old I made a skirt for my Barbie doll and designing became my hobby from then on.' She staged her first runway show at Hong Kong Fashion Week in 1997 and then the following year at Australian Fashion Week in a group show, followed by individual shows for the next two years. In 2001 the designer moved her collections to London Fashion Week and later to New York where she now shows on a regular basis to strong reviews by the likes of *Vogue, Teen Vogue, i-D, Elle* and *W.* 'There is a huge audience and fan base in New York that respond well to what we do. Out of the four main fashion weeks, New York is definitely the most suited to us in terms of personality and environment.'

In two decades Walker has grown her small label into a multi-faceted business with several diffusion brands: Karen Walker Eyewear, Karen Walker Runaway, Karen Walker Accessories and Karen Walker Paints, each of which are managed separately from the Karen Walker mainline but

1 Metallic dress, Resort 09/10

embody the same unique aesthetic and philosophy. Stocked by over 250 stores worldwide, there are also three Karen Walker stores in New Zealand and one in Taipei, with a fifth planned to open in Japan. 'You need to be adding another dimension to your business every 18 months,' she adds, which may explain the immense success of her label that remains visually engaging every season, despite the relative simplicity of her work. Walker believes her design style is 'effortless high casual,' which is an apt description of the original, unpretentious and trans-seasonal clothing that epitomises anti It-girls like Ally Sheedy in *The Breakfast Club* and Diane Keaton in *Annie Hall*. The juxtaposition of tailoring and streetwear 'is the kind of thing that interests me,' explains Walker. It is a concept adored by her celebrity following, with Björk, Sienna Miller, Claire Danes and Drew Barrymore purchasing new pieces each season. In fact,

Walker's men's style pants worn by Madonna at the MTV awards spurred an international trend and significantly propelled the Karen Walker label.

In 2007 Walker was awarded the Prix de Marie Claire award for Best Creative Talent. Not limited to her seasonal collections, Walker has collaborated with other artists around the world to refresh her work, including stylist Heathermary Jackson, director Michel Gondry and designer Henry Holland of House of Holland. As well as this, the designer established a pop-up store in The Den of New York's East Village and worked on a makeup line with Boots 17 in the UK.

So how does Walker run a highly successful, internationally recognised business from a small, isolated country? 'Technology has allowed for that,' she explains. 'It [minimises] the physical distance and time [difference], and that really is a new thing in the fashion industry. It fits with our work; we like contrast, and living in a country that is the last stop before Antarctica is not something that traditionally bodes with high fashion. I love New York, but I also love sitting in my backyard and seeing the sky.'

3 Chiffon top and silk faille skirt, S/S 09/10

4 Sweatshirt dress, S/S 09/10

5 Silk cotton shirt and pearl and
gold necklace, S/S 09/10

'THE DAY AFTER MY FIRST SHOW IN NEW
YORK THE HOME PAGE OF STYLE.COM READ
"NYC WELCOMES KAREN WALKER",
AND THAT WAS DEFINITELY ONE OF THOSE
LUMP-IN-THE-THROAT MOMENTS'
– Karen Walker

KARLA ŠPETIĆ
KARLA ŠPETIĆ

Karla Špetić believes that everything in fashion has been done before, so a unique point of view can be constructed in the way that elements are combined and contrasted. Špetić, designer of her own self-titled label, began designing as a way to overcome her shy personality. Fashion was, for Špetić, something of a dream world where she was able to escape.

Špetić was born in Dubrovnik, Croatia, before moving to Australia in 1993 as a young child to start a new life with her family. As Špetić recalls, 'When I came to Australia I was really conscious of the way I looked. I was really withdrawn and insecure and I wanted to have amazing clothes. I started playing around with garments and making things for myself, and straight after school began fashion training.' Špetić first developed her skills in a design foundation course in Queensland, before moving to Sydney to study at the TAFE Design Institute, graduating in 2005; a course that, she tells, 'was really hard and very competitive, but leads you to do the best you can. I learnt so much.'

As part of a unique initiative, Karla Špetić was one of six fashion college graduates to take part in the Graduate Store in Sydney's Strand Arcade, whereby each designer was required to stock the shelves with their collections, pay for rent and expenses, and work in the shop. This experience gave all of the designers, Špetić included, a strong grounding in retail and managing a business. 'It was a great learning experience,' says Špetić. Today, Špetić's focus is on wholesale in the domestic market. 'It's really just the beginning. I'd love to expand more when I've grown the collections and developed my work a bit more. There is so much to learn, but maybe one day I'd like to open a boutique with my

1 Cotton jersey dress, A/W 10

experience from the Graduate Store,' adds Špetić.

The growth of Špetić's brand and the increase in its popularity in a relatively short time is due in large part to the complex beauty of her work, which finds its individuality in Špetić's use of varying elements. 'Even though there is a point of difference in the clothes,' explains Špetić, 'they are still very wearable. Everything has been done before, it's just the way you put it all together. I think my point of difference is in the tailoring and the cut – maybe a sharp hourglass silhouette – but the colours and prints are very unique, too.' Indeed, Špetić's colour palette has been known to be both bold and restrained, depending on the style of the collection. Where colour is used, often it is in prints that the designer creates with an illustrator or graphic designer. 'I start with an image in my head and then research it. In the Spring/Summer 2008/2009 collection, I saw these molecular models, and the shapes of the clothes and the print used came from there. Whereas [in 2009], I was thinking a lot about my home in Croatia, and so there were a lot more of those influences in the collections. They always end up very different but gradually there are more and more similarities between them.'

'EVERYTHING HAS BEEN
DONE BEFORE, IT'S JUST
THE WAY YOU PUT IT ALL
TOGETHER'
– *Karla Spĕtić*

3 Silk crepe and
georgette dress, A/W 10

2 Silk crepe dress and
wool cardigan, A/W 10

In her work, Špetić creates a
relationship or dialogue between
the cut or style of the garment and
the print, but this is often atypical,
creating a unique proposition: where
a soft, scoop-neck summer dress
is created, it may be in a heavy,
black crocheted wool; or in soft pink
swimsuits, where the cloth may be
wrapped around the body in several
places as one continual stream. As
Špetić explains, 'I'm still developing
my aesthetic and ideas. It's often
very feminine, but not in an over-
the-top way, maybe just in the finer
details or finishes, or in the colour.
I have things that are playful and
quirky, and then other pieces that are
more refined, like a tailored blazer
or a knit sweater. I like to mix it up
and play on the hard lines mixed with
feminine ideas.'

4 Silk crepe de chine pants
and wool scarf, A/W 10

KATE SYLVESTER
KATE SYLVESTER

New Zealand designer Kate Sylvester takes much pride in her work, balancing classic tailoring and historically-steeped techniques in each collection with humour, modernity and originality. From each line in her well-established brand is wearable clothing that does not prescribe to seasonal trends, but instead remains firmly rooted in the sophisticated and independent aesthetic that is Kate Sylvester.

In association with her husband and business partner Wayne Conway, Sylvester officially launched her brand in 1993 following smaller ventures of designing and selling clothes since the age of 14. 'All I've done my whole life is make clothes,' tells Sylvester, 'right from when I was making clothes for my dolls to making clothes for myself. I've lived in dress-ups my whole life. It was when I was about 13 that I realised I could make a living out of playing.' Sylvester studied a fashion trade course before travelling to Europe where she worked under the tutelage of several big-name designers including Arabella Pollen in London and Corinne Cobson in Paris. 'I learnt so much about tailoring and making really beautiful quality clothes,' says Sylvester, the former of which was a brand designed for royalty and latter of which was wildly grunge ('of recycling and dyeing bras from the markets.'). 'The two were incredibly valuable for me.'

Upon returning to New Zealand, Sylvester and Conway together opened a small store in an Auckland back street called Sister, the space in which they sold Sylvester's burgeoning label. 'I sewed all the clothes myself, did production, designed the clothes and worked in the shop.' The store – and label – continued to grow until 1997 when they launched the Kate Sylvester name. The Kate Sylvester brand today operates three distinct lines, the

1 Silk dress and wool cardigan, A/W 10

main of which caters to women and men, a younger diffusion of the main line titled Sylvester and, more recently, eyewear and footwear. The business, including four retail stores and wholesale throughout Australasia and the US, also employs 20 staff. And Sylvester is most happy with the development that has ensued since her humble beginnings. As she tells, 'I just love being able to design the complete package, covering everything from shoes and eyewear to the boyfriend of my female customer.'

Sylvester attributes her success in part to Australian and New Zealand Fashion Weeks, which she tells, are 'really great whenever we do it, and incredibly beneficial... a great platform.' Although Sylvester's shows haven't come without their controversy – including a front page *Sydney Morning Herald* article in 2008 regarding the use of war medals worn by models in

her Spring/Summer 2008/2009 show – they are, typically, a much revered event on both calendars for their innovative use of staging, production and styling. Significantly, styling plays a large part in communicating the Kate Sylvester aesthetic or concept. The concepts, Sylvester tells, 'often come out of books, because I read a lot. I've done a lot of collections based on Jackson Pollock, Gustav Klimt, Vanessa Beecroft... so art comes in quite often. Even music – I did an entire collection inspired by a Nick Cave song once. I love

2 Silk jacket, A/W 04

'I LOVE MAKING A THEME FOR THE COLLECTION'
– Kate Sylvester

two extremes I play with.' Conway is responsible for creating the prints used in the collections. 'In *Take A Hike,* for example, we did a fantastic wood grain print that he designed.'

The Kate Sylvester brand has most recently established a sustainability policy, which includes a commitment to onshore production and the employment of an ever-expanding collection of ethical and organic fabric options. As Sylvester explains, 'we try to consider impact on the environment and ethical implications when making decisions. We are always first and foremost a fashion brand but we are trying to be a responsible one. I don't think this is an issue limited to the fashion industry. I don't want people to turn into rabid greenies, but I believe that any change people can make is for the better.' Sourcing organic cotton yarn from Europe which is independently certified, Sylvester then has it knitted into fabric in a New Zealand mill, where all her garments are created. 'I don't advocate spending. I advocate spending responsibly,' she adds. 'If we all stop buying disposable fashion then we're helping the environment.'

making a theme for the collection.' In an ever-evolving combination of design, form and function, Sylvester fuses such ideas with highly wearable wardrobe basics, such as simple jersey summer dresses, cotton collared safari-style shirts and belted, lightweight trench coats.

In creating energy in each collection, Sylvester mashes together couture tailoring techniques with sportswear or more unstructured pieces, harking back to her training in fashion. 'They are

'THE BEAUTY OF THE
FASHION INDUSTRY
IS THAT EVERYONE IS
ALWAYS ON THE
LOOKOUT FOR
SOMETHING FRESH
AND NEW'
– Kirrily Johnston

1 Double silk tulle
dress, S/S 09/10

2 Jersey t-shirt,
leather vest, cotton
twill shorts and modal
leggings, S/S 09/10

collection and she took it on. It really all began from there.' As Johnston was running the store, she merchandised her product in the store windows alongside luxury brand imports, which slowly attracted a following of customers and other retailers. Johnston relocated to Sydney in 2000 and presented her first complete collection to excellent acclaim. 'It can be hard to get that initial bit of recognition, but once I had people's attention I found they were interested and supportive. The beauty of the fashion industry is that everyone is always on the lookout for something fresh and new.' What Johnston creates each season is just that.

Johnston's style is distinctly unique and a defining aspect of her business. Inspired not by trends or drawing on European clothing influences, Johnston's ongoing inspiration is that of national costume, something she explores with each collection.
'I find it beautiful and compelling,' she says. 'And growing up in a country where it doesn't really exist made it all the more exotic to me when I was growing up. I can't get enough of cultural learning and I think this feeds a lot of what I do.' Johnston's studio is

something of an inspiration, too, in a small, light-filled attic above her Paddington store that she uses to sketch her collections. Filled with drawings, found images and clippings, Johnston spends time each season in the space where she can creatively breathe and reflect, subsequently creating a mood board from which she then draws firmer ideas about structure, textiles and form. It's an aesthetic that she describes as 'elegant and directional.'

Consisting of separates in neutral colour palettes of silks, wools and knits, a Kirrily Johnston collection is likely to consist of Ghandi-inspired harem pants, knitted multi-wrap-around tops, long, asymmetrically-cut leather vests and jackets and bandage-style wrapped sandals. 'Draping is really big for me. I do a lot of work directly on the body and mannequin to create unique shapes and patterns. I also love volume and unusual silhouettes, which allow me to play with proportion." And although pattern isn't usually present in Johnston's work, patchwork often is, giving a base of beige and white a strong injection of bold colours like peach and blood orange. Johnston's customer does not fall into a distinct age group, but 'has a willingness to invest and often travels. She is not only she, either... we introduced [in 2009] a unisex line, and we've had many men coming in and buying my drapey knitwear and loose tights.'

Johnston is also a strong supporter of the Australian fashion industry, noting that Australian Fashion Week has not only been a positive exercise for her brand but 'a very important event that has put many Australian labels on the map [globally] and contributed enormously to local industry. I take my hat off to Simon Lock for starting it up – who else would have taken on such a massive project? We have all benefited, including the community, not just the industry. I wish more people would appreciate it.' This attitude is in keeping with Johnston's focus on the Asian market, which she finds logistically easier than the northern hemisphere. As well as operating a wholesale business, Johnston maintains boutique stores in Sydney and Melbourne. It is Johnston, too, that manages the business, 'driving the direction and overseeing everything.'

'I try to stay true to what I want and what I feel customers want,' she says of her continued relevance and growing status in the market. 'I am constantly researching new avenues, new techniques and new ways of doing things. I am ultimately very dedicated to what I do.' And with what she does being ultimately creative, it is something Johnston would like to continue to build upon. 'I want to collaborate more, to paint more, to make films. It's all achievable because my goals are more about lifestyle than dollars.'

3 (Both wear) brushed cotton capes, modal leggings and pony skin boots, A/W 10

KONSTANTINA MITTAS
KONSTANTINA MITTAS

Designer Konstantina Mittas does not have any formal training in fashion design, creating her collections intuitively and based on shapes and forms that attract her senses. From her unassuming studio and showroom in Sydney's Chippendale, Mittas manages all aspects of her business – from design and production to marketing and sales.

As Mittas tells, 'I have been making things for as long as I can remember. I was always attracted to fashion.' This passion led Mittas to work in fashion wholesaling. At one point in her career, the young Mittas found herself unemployed and with little hope of finding a new job imminently. 'I had made something a little crazy to wear out with my friends, and I had so many girls coming up to me asking what I was wearing. I just started taking people's names, numbers and money. I was dealing fashion. I really had no money at this stage, and so would use the money from five singlets to make ten more.' It's humbling in such a large industry to hear such stories of fashion being created for the sake of it being appreciated and worn. 'It's very much like-attracts-like,' agrees the designer. And since this point three years ago – with singlets and denim Mittas would paint and embellish with scrap and vintage fabric – her craft-like aesthetic has remained, albeit in more of a structured and formalised manner. 'I got to a point where I was physically exhausted. I couldn't do this hand embellishment any more, so I started introducing woven fabrics and other pieces.' From here, the Konstantina Mittas label was created.

Mittas has taught herself everything she knows today about designing and managing a fashion brand. Mittas wonders, 'I don't even know how I know things. It's like with an artist; I just can't explain how I know about design.

1 Cotton velvet pants and top and silk organza overdress, A/W 10

The designer's Spring/Summer 2009/2010 collection *The Strangeness* explores themes of industrial femininity, with vivid canary yellow singlets and dresses in perforated jersey, playing against high-waisted, ballooning skirts that sculpt narrowly to the knees. An earlier collection, *In Flight,* takes a more literal cue, incorporating sharply structured shoulders that resemble a bird's wings, and light, crepe silk that wraps sensually around the upper body before billowing out into a flowing trail that catches the wind. And yet despite the conceptual nature of Mittas' work, absent is any sense of gimmick or connotation of costume, avoided by the designer's use of quality fabrics (jersey, cotton, silk, leather, wool) and hand finishing that brings a couture-like quality to the construction of the garments.

That instinct is not something you can be taught. Training is great in that it makes you aware of tools, machines and resources, and you have the opportunity to just be creative.' That said, Mittas' position today, as one of Australia's leading avant-garde designers, is testament to her individual spirit. 'You can learn as you go if you're passionate,' believes Mittas.

'I think my angle or approach is quite artistic. You're working with something in your hands – which is really quite a sculptural approach to fashion. And that comes out in the clothing.' Indeed, Mittas' clothing has something of a sculptural quality, and often to unusual and surprising effect.

Mittas finds her inspiration in art forms, shapes and light; elements she believes are natural as a result of growing up in Australia. 'There is a slight futuristic element to my work, but because of its construction and shapes it is still quite organic. It's quite a modern way of thinking.' Mittas attributes

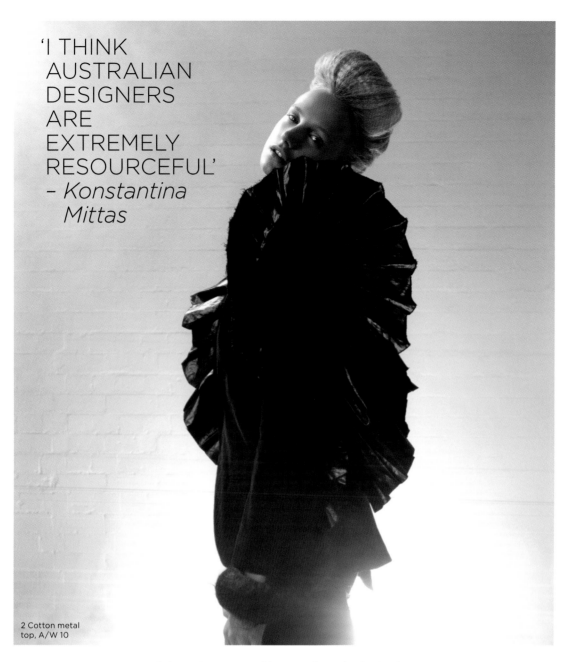

'I THINK
AUSTRALIAN
DESIGNERS
ARE
EXTREMELY
RESOURCEFUL'
– *Konstantina
Mittas*

2 Cotton metal
top, A/W 10

part of the uniqueness of her work to the limited resources available in
Australia. 'If you want to do a button or hardware like a zip, you're limited
in your choices as we're a smaller, younger country than, say, Europe.
I guess that's what happens when you're creative. If you can't have
something, you'll just make something else. I could do a whole collection
with just two fabrics if I needed to. I'm more focused on the actual design.'

Although the Australian market is quite small, particularly in its offering
of conceptual fashion design, Mittas has remained true to her vision and
aesthetic. This unwavering commitment to her creativity has led the
designer to gain the respect of media and niche retailers alike. As she
explains, 'I just do my own thing, and you can have anyone in any age
group buying into it.'

3 Wool dress,
A/W 10

KSUBI
GEORGE GORROW AND DAN SINGLE

Ksubi began, according to designers George Gorrow and Dan Single, as 'a big group of friends inspiring each other. We were looking for a project to unite us all: bums, drunks, poets, photographers, artists.' And today, a decade after its inception as a collection of distressed denim, Ksubi remains representative of the epoch through its innovative, collective and humorous approach to fashion.

'We had always talked about a clothing line,' explains Gorrow, 'and agreed to set up the label as a platform for everything we were into. Dan Single, Oska Wright, Paul Wilson, myself and some others locked ourselves in Oska's garage studio for three days until we had developed an idea for the label. From there, we just explored the medium of fashion until we settled on a first collection.' Despite the fact that the Ksubi designers were experimental with their dress sense and grew up in the broader creative fields, they were, as Gorrow tells, 'complete strangers to the fashion industry.' And yet refreshingly, Ksubi's non-conformist approach to fashion was what gained them such considerable press coverage and, ultimately, their position as Australia's avant-garde heroes.

In 2000 (their first year), Ksubi secured some free exhibition space at Australian Fashion Week, whereby they presented, after only days of creation, denim that had been mutated (for lack of a better word) with garden tools and whatever else they could get their hands on. This initial presentation secured the fledgling designers with several large orders and a lot of (mixed) press. Not to be outdone by their exploitation of denim jeans, Gorrow and Single created a stronger, fuller collection the following year, unleashing hundreds of rats onto the runway in their

presentation of roughly perforated clothing. Indeed, Ksubi positioned themselves as the rats of Australian fashion, gradually eating away at the convention of catwalk and the relationship between designer and collection. And while the pair have been criticised for their theatrical antics – Sydney Harbour boat parties whereby models 'walked the plank' into the water, for example – it can't be denied that Ksubi has remained true to its roustabout, non-traditional fashion background and all that the work stands for.

According to Gorrow, the use of shows and installations is a means of communication through which to express their singular vision. 'Every idea is different, and is conceived in a different way from the last. We try to keep the spirit of the idea and don't let reality get in the way or water it down. Our shows are really multi-mediated

– from the music and set design, which we see as installation art – to the concept and the clothes. They all play an equal part, none of them dominating the other.' The relaxed, ironic and sexy Ksubi collection – casual wear, surfwear, eyewear, jewellery, shoes and denim – is consistently comfortable and timelessly relevant. Fashion, the Ksubi designers believe, is moving incredibly fast, and they're fine with that. 'Everything goes in cycles, but they're getting shorter and shorter. Eventually fashion will be a mix of every era.' Gorrow believes that the Ksubi aesthetic is 'not worth talking about,' in that while it remains true to their identity, each season it stems from 'something we are getting right into. It might be a style of music, an artist that we are infatuated with, or one (or all) of our friends. It could be one line of a poem that opens up the thoughts that end up slamming you headfirst

2 (From left) cotton shirt and denim shorts; denim shirt and denim jeans, S/S 08 (northern hemisphere)

into your concept.' In this way, Ksubi's customer base is as broad as the inspiration is endless.

It's not often that an Australian brand has the power to cross international borders, particularly with the impact Ksubi had when it launched. Such hype has spurred artistic collaborations with such international visionaries as Jeremy Scott and Richard Nicoll. And although the international market is one of great interest for the designers, particularly as they grow the structured fashion element of their collections and with a growing stockist list, the Australian market remains the most important. 'Guys here dress cooler than men overseas,' explain the designers. 'Every time we get home from long overseas trips we're always impressed by what we have in Australia.'

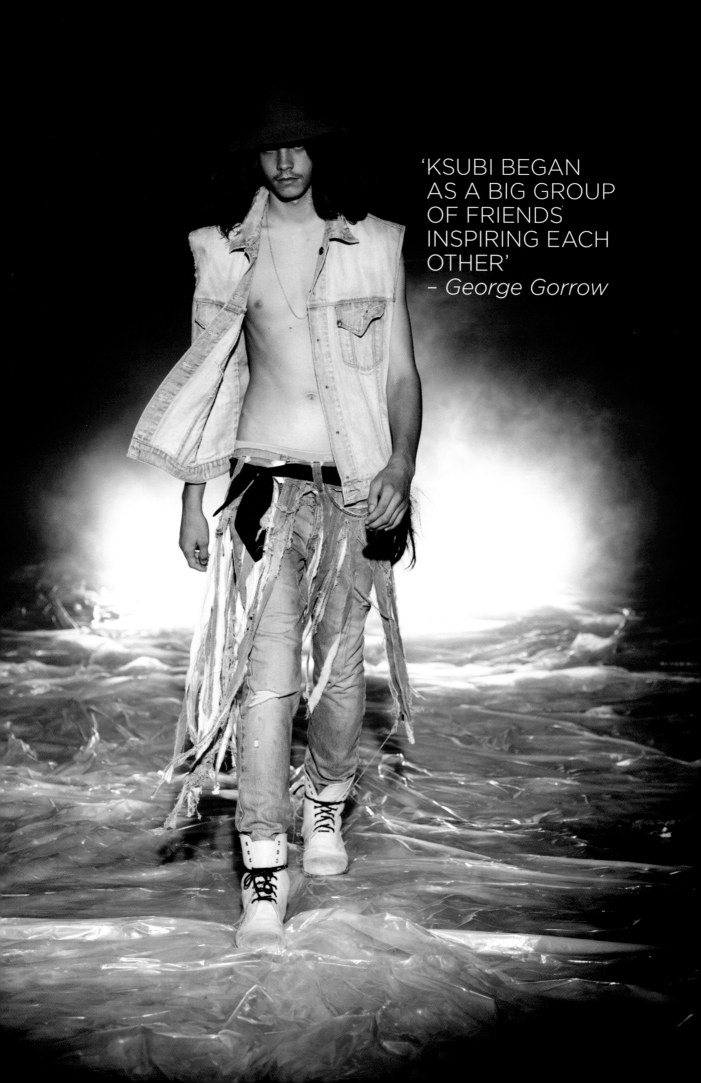

'KSUBI BEGAN
AS A BIG GROUP
OF FRIENDS
INSPIRING EACH
OTHER'
– *George Gorrow*

LEONA EDMISTON
LEONA EDMISTON

If there is a story to be told about the growth of Australian fashion, Leona Edmiston is a fitting narrator. In 1983, straight out of fashion school, Edmiston launched the wildly popular Morrissey Edmiston brand with fellow Australian designer Peter Morrissey. 'It seemed that anything was possible,' Edmiston tells today. 'It seemed it was possible to start with no money, no marketing plan, and in a very modest way. A lot of people were doing that at the time.' Splitting with Morrissey in 1997, Edmiston took with her lessons learnt and launched her current label, Leona Edmiston, in 2001. Today, she is known fondly as the Queen of Frocks.

Studying fashion at the then East Sydney Technical College, Edmiston found herself in the swelling industry that was Australian fashion in the early 1980s. Though fashion wasn't always what the designer planned to do. 'I've always loved playing with style, but I enjoyed playing with houses and home stuff just as much. It was something I always enjoyed but never gave it too much thought.' Without too much thought, also, was the birth of Morrissey Edmiston. 'Fashion was less sophisticated [at that time]. We opened our first retail store almost instantly – a cooperative with five other designers. Lots of people were doing screenprinting, and it was very hands-on – a bit cottage-like by today's standards.' The success of the label, however, was far from small, and is remembered today by fashion diehards and average punters alike. Indeed, many people can still recall the heyday of Michael Hutchence, Kylie Minogue and Helena Christensen wearing the clothes with pride and sex appeal. 'It was all very exciting!'

'I learnt a lot of lessons during those years – it was my education, in a way. And so when I launched my own business I had a very definite

idea of what it should be.'
Most importantly was the type
of collections produced: in size
they were much smaller than
those of Morrissey Edmiston and
were designed specifically for
women. Perhaps most defining of
Edmiston's career is her penchant
for – and obvious talent for creating
– feminine dresses. 'It was the thing
I always enjoyed doing the most,'
she explains. 'When it came to
setting up my business I thought 'I
am going to focus completely on
what I enjoy', and it's proven to be
successful.' She notes here that in
2001 the 'frock' had disappeared,
with fashion lending itself more to
separates, but that in recent years
it has become very popular again,
particularly so in Australia. 'It gave
me a few years to work out shapes
so I could take advantage when
it hit with a bang. I love making
frocks and hopefully I can forever.'
If her hopefulness hints at her
worry about the economic climate,
Edmiston need not worry, for her
business has grown successfully
into a multi-branded empire in
under a decade. In this business,
Edmiston manages the creative

1 Jersey dress, A/W 10

division while her husband works as
the company's managing director,
handling finance and logistics.

Showing initially at Australian
Fashion Week – which Edmiston
believes is 'a great start and
fantastic support' (but doesn't fall
within her buying/selling timelines)
– Leona Edmiston was born.
'Retail has always been very
important to us, and we've now
grown to 18 retail outlets, as well as
international sales and concessions
in Myer department stores. For us
it has always been broad and we
never believed in limiting the ways
we can get the product out there.'

2 Jersey and silk
chiffon dress, A/W 10

'THE AIM IS TO TELL A
SUCCINCT STORY'
– *Leona Edmiston*

Having her own stores allows Edmiston to communicate directly with her
customers and gives her complete buying control.

Inspired by the women who wear her clothes, Edmiston has successfully
added several diffusions and lines to her business, including hosiery,
bags, candles, shoes and sunglasses, as well as a more affordable line,
Leona Edmiston Ruby, for Myer. Not merely a commercial venture, these
lines represent the quintessential Leona Edmiston customer: 'I haven't
wanted to diversify within apparel, and so for a woman who doesn't buy
a dress every day but still loves the label we've added extensions to the
frock range. The aim is to tell a succinct story.' At the core of this story is
her main range of apparel, which Edmiston believes is 'feminine but not
fussy.' Created predominantly from jersey, the designer works with certain
European mills each season to create signature prints, those which have
defined her as a designer in the international market place. 'I love prints
and use lots of them,' she boasts.

3 Jersey dress, A/W 10

LIFEWITHBIRD
BRIDGET McCALL AND NICHOLAS VAN MESSNER

When stylist and photographer Bridget (Bird) McCall met fashion designer Nicholas Van Messner in 2002 it was 'a really natural progression to do something together', with the two creatives sharing a similar design aesthetic. LIFEwithBIRD was established that year as an accessories label selling leathergoods and bags, and soon after branched into clothing, retaining the individuality and modernity of their original line.

Messner's initial application to study fashion design at RMIT University was rejected. Feeling cheated after putting such energy into building a portfolio, Messner returned and bullied his way into the course. Successfully graduating three years later, the designer worked for quirky menswear label Maiike where he honed his technical ability. McCall trained at the Photography Studies College in Melbourne before moving to London where she collaborated on magazine shoots for *The Face* and *i-D* magazines, returning to Australia to work as an accessories agent where she met Messner.

As Messner tells of LIFEwithBIRD, 'I'm very structural, looking at the technical side of it and thinking in 3D. We work well together because Bridget comes from a style background. What is great about fashion is that with everything you design you have to work out a new way to do it, and that's what drives you.' This sensibility of construction is evident in the clothes of the label, which are edgy, modern and well-cut. Both designers agree on the unique categorisation of 'luxury sportswear'. 'We're not afraid to put a sequined sports jacket over a pair of jeans for the day or a soft, feminine dress with a tailored tuxedo jacket. We love the contrast,' explains McCall.

The designers create their collections by building upon their work from previous seasons. 'We quite often grab a whole bunch of pieces and hack them apart, pin them together, Bridget tries them on and we play with them,' explains Messner of the process. This unusual practise saw LIFEwithBIRD nominated for the Tiffany & Co. Designer of the Year Award in 2006 and gain numerous high calibre international stockists. 'We probably sell more in Japan than we do in Australia, largely due to the fact we have great stores stocking us there. It's really interesting; the Japanese people tend to wear five of your pieces all at once, which is amazing but you can't imagine it happening in Melbourne or Sydney.' This in mind, the duo has no desire for market saturation, believing the mega brand to be dead. 'The market is so fragmented,' notes Messner. 'Luxury is in the niche label.'

'WE WERE DETERMINED TO SUCCEED
AND THERE WAS NO EXIT PLAN.
IT WAS REALLY ALL OR NOTHING'
– *Bridget McCall*

2 Dupion silk and metallic jersey dress, metallic
jersey bra and nylon shorts, S/S 07/08

LISA HO
LISA HO

Lisa Ho is one of the most recognisable names in Australian fashion. Launching in 1982, her signature design aesthetic has remained constant despite trends and market changes. Ho, who worked fleetingly for another label after college before designing her own collection, believes the most notable change about fashion in almost 30 years is how its significance has increased.

Upon graduating from Sydney's TAFE Design Institute in 1981, Ho worked in the industry for a year, despising the male-controlled, corporate world of fashion in Australia at the time. 'I absolutely loathed the people and the culture,' she recalls today. 'It was really staid and very male-dominated and not very inspiring – just very limiting.' Although, like many of Australia's designers, it is claimed that Ho began her own design career at Paddington Markets, she notes that it was 'literally only five weeks, and to be honest they weren't that helpful. I started wholesaling pretty much straight away, cutting, patternmaking and doing everything myself in those early days. It was a lot of hard work.' Work that has, evidently, paid off. Ho's business today employs 120 staff, working in her Sydney studio and also in her 12 stores throughout Australia. As well as this, the Lisa Ho label is stocked in 250 boutiques throughout the world, including concession stores within department store David Jones.

That Ho is running an international venture from Australia – a country that was not at all considered fashion forward when she began – doesn't seem of interest to her. 'I think the idea of Australian culture in clothing is really overrated... If you're a creative person, then it doesn't matter what country you're based in. We're not designing dresses with boomerangs on

1 Beaded silk t-shirt,
leather jacket and silk and
emu feather skirt, A/W 10

[them].' This notion, Ho continues, has been supported by the digital revolution and the introduction of the internet to business. 'It's really sped things up,' she believes. 'It's opened many doors; made it easier for us to seek out new products or share information, to communicate internationally... it's been an incredible tool.'

However, Ho isn't preoccupied with the internet as a source of inspiration. Each collection, she tells, begins with a theme. 'For my latest collection,' Ho explains, 'I've been influenced by one particular painting by Terry Rogers, *The Girl is Muse.*' From this point, Ho creates a mood board around her theme or idea. 'That for me is how a collection evolves. Of course, I've got a particular style or handwriting, so that just develops naturally with the inspiration.' Ho and her creative team also design unique prints used in each collection, 'and so I've got colour references, texture references, the type of jewellery I might want to present with the collection. It's everything. We'll say "she's living this type of lifestyle and so she'd have this type of thing in her wardrobe."'

Ho draws analysis from her retail network on what styles and garments are popular in each season and city, and this ultimately influences the style and form of future collections. 'Until I started opening retail stores I had to rely on wholesale customers, which is a little frustrating because you're at the mercy of what the stores are going to buy from you, and they don't often represent the brand how you would like it. Having your own stores gives you the freedom to represent the collection in its entirety.' Ho follows some structure based on sales, but still presents a full range that tells a story and explains the Lisa Ho aesthetic. 'You need to deliver a full collection. That's what sets a true designer apart from someone who is just making clothing to sell.'

In building the image and public perception of her label, Ho attributes part of her success to Australian Fashion Week.

'I THINK THE IMPORTANCE OF FASHION HAS INCREASED'
– Lisa Ho

2 (From left) beaded silk t-shirt, leather jacket and silk and emu feather skirt; fur gilet and viscose raffia dress; leather vest, beaded silk jacket and nylon dress; wool twill dress; studded leather bolero, fur gilet and nylon dress; silk and feather cape, nylon bodysuit, silk tank and acetate print pants; leather bolero and silk and ostrich feather dress; silk satin organza dress, A/W 10

'It's brought the industry together and really catapulted Australian designers more than any other vehicle. We've seen fashion go to another level, and people understand that fashion is a very powerful tool and can use it to make themselves feel better or present themselves in a certain way. I think the importance of fashion has increased.' And as fashion's importance has increased in society and culture, Ho believes the manufacturing industry behind it has changed, too. 'Some of my suppliers are still the same as when I was a student, and some have changed. We produce about half of our collection in Australia. If you have a complicated garment, there just isn't the workforce or the skills to get it done here, which is a pity.'

Ho's collections are distinctly feminine and wearable, consisting most notably of dresses and separates that straddle the line between formal and casual elegance. 'I use a lot of silk chiffons, and I try to use natural fibres as much as possible. I only use things that are soft to the skin.' And as Ho tells that while the style changes each season, her collections err on the side of being sexy. This, she reveals, is made possible by using high quality fabrics and, where possible, something with a little stretch. 'Even a silk with a bit of Lycra makes a garment more comfortable and sit well on the body.'

3 Printed silk dress, A/W 10

LOVER
NIC BRIAND AND SUSIEN CHONG

Partners in business and in love, Nic Briand and Susien Chong believe their success is largely attributed to luck. Not so much in way of design – for they strongly believe in their work, from where it derives and for what it stands – but in terms of building a brand and breaking into the fashion industry whilst staying true to their philosophies and unique practice.

Briand and Chong established Lover in 2000 in the most humble of manners. 'We lived about 100 metres away from Bondi Markets,' explains Chong of early Lover days, 'and we would cram all the clothes we had made and racks into our little Honda Civic, and Nic couldn't even fit in the car so would walk down and meet me there. We did this for about three months over summer before one of the buyers from The Corner Shop came down and bought our clothes in a wholesale capacity, so we started a bigger wholesale network.' What the fledgling designers found most interesting about this point in time was that the style of clothing was extremely DIY, as Briand coins it. 'Everyone was customising t-shirts, jeans, singlets, putting corsages on jackets and t-shirts. sass & bide and Ksubi created that aesthetic and did it so well, and there was just so many people at the markets emulating it.' That Lover veered away from this style did not hinder them. Rather, their puff-sleeved preppy shirts, lace blouses, and neat-look clothing found a customer base that craved something different. 'It really gave us confidence and showed us there was a market for what we were doing; that people were willing to go in the opposite direction,' says Briand.

The luck that Briand and Chong refer to is in the timing. 'It was at that time when young designers were really on the cusp,' recalls Chong.

1 Campaign, S/S 08/09

'A lot of young designers were having success at an early stage and it worked as good timing for us starting out on our own.' Briand had worked in youth marketing and advertising after studying fine arts at the University of New South Wales, and worked on accounts such as Lee Jeans and Tropfest, whilst Chong, a design graduate from University of Technology, Sydney, was working as a design assistant for Zimmermann. Having been a couple already for five years, the pair began working together on projects through Zimmermann, realising that it would be possible to work together on something of their own. This period, they tell, was spurred by adrenalin. 'There was a lot going on and a lot of attention on you as a young label, but it doesn't matter that you're doing the long hours and it's just the two of you, because it's so exciting,' says Briand. 'It's all about the creativity, and we wouldn't change anything for those first few years.' Chong continues: 'And it's about the ideas! You don't think of sitting down and doing your tax, which is what consumes you later on: the business. You have more responsibility as time goes on: rent to pay, staff to pay. We try to find a balance between creativity and business.'

Perhaps one of the most powerful tools that assisted Lover in its

2 Cotton shirt and
wool shorts, A/W 05

base, connecting with likeminded creatives. 'A lot of people write it off as time-wasting, but you're creating a relationship with people that are on your wavelength. It perpetuates [discussion] about the brand, and hopefully that will lead someone to walk into a shop and buy Lover at some point in the future.'

Lover staged three runway shows early in their history, but now promote their new seasons online through a visual lookbook. The statistics, they say, are on the incline and sales peak around the time of upload. With a successful online store, the internet is most definitely an important tool for Lover. While Briand believes the increasing prevalence of the internet is ironing out cultural differences in fashion and style, Lover has remained true to its own aesthetic and concept. The label's fiercely loyal customer base has stood by this and, today, recognises certain films, people and music as 'very Lover'; something the designers find a great compliment. 'Someone said that Lover is an appreciation of aesthetics,' says Briand. 'It really can range from so many things, but there is this thread of beauty running through it. When you see it, you know it.' As Chong continues, 'you can see how our business is structured: it's grown organically,

development and growth was the internet. Having established their label when the internet was being embraced by the populace as an everyday tool, Lover unknowingly launched a culture that formed online. As Chong tells, 'most people didn't know how to use it to their full advantage or disadvantage. I guess we were just lucky.' In 2004, Lover was one of few Australian designers to have their own website. By chance, Briand created a MySpace account for Lover, following the lead of bands and musicians. 'Our philosophy was to market [the label] like a band; a collection like an album,' he says, and this created a strong dialogue with an ever-expanding customer it's grassroots, we still feel independent. How we run the business goes into that big pot of how people perceive Lover. It's important for us to do what we believe in because people always come back to that and respect that it doesn't change gears and follow other trends.'

While each season varies in terms of styles and garments, the pair explain that they attempt to fulfil every category so as to provide a well-rounded collection and tell a story. 'We had a lot of success with a short short a few seasons ago,' says Chong, 'and then they were everywhere, and now we've found success with blazers. From there we'll create a few more next season, developing and reinterpreting it over a period. We don't like to do it all at once. Lover has always been a slow burner.' Often, Lover have been ahead of the trend curve – such as with bodysuits, which the majority of buyers laughed at several years ago – but have persisted for seasons until customers have come around. As well as casual separates, Lover introduced a swimwear range in 2007, consisting of both one and two-piece costumes in textured knit fabrics and with detailing, reflecting their unique approach to fashion in the mainline. Such developments demonstrate Lover's ability to grow whilst retaining their recognisable

'WE'VE CREATED THIS CULTURE AROUND THE BRAND AND NOW PEOPLE CAN IDENTIFY THINGS AS 'LOVER'. IT'S A FEELING AND SENSE OF COMMUNITY'
– *Susien Chong*

3 French lace dress, S/S 09/10

and beloved aesthetic. As Briand explains, 'you have to evolve, you have to screw up the canvas. Once you know how to do it, you can abstract it and change it.'

MANNING CARTELL
CHERYL, GABRIELLE AND VANESSA MANNING

Sisters Cheryl, Gabrielle and Vanessa Manning together form Sydney-based womenswear label Manning Cartell. The Manning sisters believe that working together is their winning formula for their consistently well-balanced, well-formed and beautifully executed collections. 'Each of us brings our own individual experience and skill to the brand, and the combination of different skills creates Manning Cartell,' they explain. This collaborative approach to both design and business has allowed Manning Cartell to strongly position itself in the Australian and international markets.

Vanessa and Gabrielle both studied design at the School of Visual Arts in Sydney, while Cheryl studied at Wiska Listans Haute Couture Academy as well as the TAFE Design Institute. From a very young age, the three tell, they were taught to use a sewing machine by their mother, and would take turns in producing clothes for themselves and each other. Vanessa describes this training as 'working our way up.' Since launching in 2006, the label has enjoyed considerable growth, with retail stores in Sydney's Strand Arcade, Paddington and Melbourne, and strong wholesale distribution throughout the Asia Pacific region. Gabrielle attributes their initial break into the industry largely to 'the help of our fantastic PR agent Golightly.' 'Fashion is all about momentum; new talent in this industry is always exciting,' adds Cheryl.

For Manning Cartell, Australian Fashion Week has been a 'very worthwhile and positive event that has really helped to create brand awareness for us,' says Cheryl. Participating in the event has earned the label great press exposure. Their third and most recent store, in Melbourne, was opened

1 Metallic
polyester
dress,
A/W 10

Inspired by fabric, artwork, detailed finishes and trimmings, Manning Cartell design for a 'new generation of free-spirited, independent, style-conscious women.' The techniques used in their work are centred predominantly around fabric, shape and volume, juxtaposing different fabrics, and washing fabrics to create a slightly worn feel. This idea is evident in, for example, a high round-necked mesh singlet paired with a high-waisted shift skirt in a heavier, more structured cotton; or a peplum-style dress, with its ballooning vertical folds, contrasted by its one-shouldered top that skews the direction of the fabric. In each collection, Manning Cartell provide a considered range of pieces relevant for various occasions and styles, from structured, sheer blouses with pocket and cuff detailing, to minimal long-sleeved wool dresses.

following the success of the two Sydney stores, which are 'the perfect canvas to showcase our collections in full.' Internationally, the trio are researching various markets to find the best fit for their style and brand.

The Manning Cartell aesthetic has quickly earned the brand huge popularity, for each collection delivers trend-inspired, innovative and imaginative pieces – a style the designers describe as 'relaxed, edgy elegance.' A contradiction in terms, the clothes feature traditionally contrasting elements in fresh new ways, providing a unique point of view.

The designers manage their business together, which they find imperative for finding and exploring new opportunities to grow the brand and to build relationships with their customers. In this vein they aim for worldwide expansion in the near future, first with wholesale accounts and later by opening boutiques to showcase the Manning Cartell world.

'THREE IS THE MAGIC NUMBER... EACH OF US BRINGS OUR OWN INDIVIDUAL EXPERIENCE AND SKILL TO THE BRAND AND THE COMBINATION OF DIFFERENT SKILLS CREATES MANNING CARTELL'
– *Vanessa Manning*

2 Silk crepe de chine dress with hand-beaded detail, A/W 10

3 Modal and acrylic top
with sequin detail, faux fur
coat and cotton washed
denim pants, A/W 10

MARNIE SKILLINGS
MARNIE SKILLINGS

'When I was young I didn't think fashion design was an option as a career,' says Marnie Skillings from her boutique in Sydney's eastern suburbs. 'I grew up in a pretty alternative environment in Lismore and wanted to be involved with the art world but was never sure how.' Despite her isolated beginnings, Marnie Skillings has become a household name in Australian fashion. She is known for her feminine and whimsical clothes that are distinctly wearable, making use of natural fabrics like silk and wool.

Skillings' degree in fine arts, majoring in printmaking, led her to study fashion design at the TAFE Design Institute. Upon graduating, the young designer took a short break before launching her namesake label with a small range of four pieces. This first collection, as part of a group show at Australian Fashion Week in 2000, demonstrated Skillings' masterful ability to combine cut, colour, print and texture, creating a natural, feminine and accessible aesthetic. From this point, the designer's sales and recognition have grown each season. Drawing inspiration from memories, Skillings is the sole designer behind her label. 'Each season I start thinking about something and then spend time in the library or at a gallery to develop the idea; I then spend days looking at fabrics and designing prints.' The majority of her work is produced in Australia, as she feels that local production is not only more ethical but provides greater opportunity to control the end result. This attitude has seen Skillings earn a reputation for high quality over the past decade. A point of difference for Skillings is her use of natural fabrics, such as washed silk and Italian merino wool. Skillings also designs her own prints for the textiles, ensuring originality.

1 Wool cashmere jacket
and skirt, A/W 10

In 2006 Skillings won the Pantene Young Woman of the Year Award in the fashion category, which she describes as 'very surprising! I didn't even think many people would know who I was, so it was completely bizarre.' The award may well have been a confidence boost for the young designer, who opened her own boutique the next year and gained several international stockists. The boutique environment has presented many challenges to the designer, such as running a business, which was completely new to Skillings. 'As a wholesaler the boutique dictates what the public will see of your collection,' she says. 'I'd always had the aim to show things I wanted, with all the extra bits and pieces we had discovered along the way, and so when the [boutique] space came up it felt like a natural progression.' As the designer tells, 'it's been a slow, comfortable process, which is how I wanted to make a business.' Skillings finds that young designers are luckier now than in the past, as there is a 'real interest in what's happening in the industry. It's no longer just a few big names, and the industry is excited about and supportive of new labels.'

2 Wool cashmere jacket, cotton
top and silk skirt, A/W 10

'YOU GET TO A
STAGE WHERE
YOU ARE LESS
TERRIFIED OF
WHAT OTHER
PEOPLE THINK
OF YOU AND
YOUR WORK,
AND THAT'S
AN AMAZING
FEELING OF
EMPOWERMENT'
– *Marnie Skillings*

MATERIALBYPRODUCT
SUSAN DIMASI AND CHANTAL KIRBY

MATERIALBYPRODUCT is one of Australia's only fashion businesses that can call themselves a house, in the European sense, as opposed to just a brand or label. Indeed, its creators Susan Dimasi and Chantal Kirby shy away from the term 'brand'. MATERIALBYPRODUCT is developed through the creation of a unique technical language and approach to manufacturing in their Melbourne-based studio and workroom. Dimasi studied at RMIT University before seeking private tuition to learn patternmaking and tailoring. After this, Dimasi worked several jobs in both Australia and London where she was able to immerse herself in the construction of clothing to learn traditional techniques, giving her the knowledge to not only utilise them in her own practice but to explore and challenge them. Dimasi is currently working towards a PhD that explores reproduction, customisation and authenticity in fashion today. Kirby began as Dimasi's assistant whilst studying a Bachelor of Arts in Fashion Design at RMIT University. Upon graduation in 2004, Kirby and Dimasi became partners, furthering their design relationship and continuing to grow and develop MATERIALBYPRODUCT.

Dimasi and Kirby are inspired and driven by fashion and the challenge of creating pieces that are relevant and beautiful. However, the work of MATERIALBYPRODUCT stems far further than the creation of garments, for each piece or collection is extensively researched and developed so that it carries a greater message, statement or relevance. 'There is an amazing depth in what we're producing,' explains Dimasi, 'so it's not just a collection. It is an entire process.' This process that Dimasi refers to is the establishment of the MATERIALBYPRODUCT workroom. 'When we started our studio we simultaneously started a workroom, and we did

1 & 2 Silk georgette flat
A-line maxi scarf, S/S 09/10

that because we set out to create our own language, and we set out to create this language through technique. So we have interrogated the concept of the brand: the fundamentals of making a garment being the way you cut the cloth, the way you join the cloth and the way you mark the cloth. From there our language evolves.'

Dimasi and Kirby's desire to create a unique signature and explore manufacturing techniques was born out of frustration at limits of the Australian industry. As Dimasi continues, 'the manufacturing culture in Australia is not one where you can collaborate. It's changed a bit now because we have a bit more ability to ask and we can choose people we're asking, but in the earlier days if you approached someone with something you wanted to do, they'd say 'this is what we do and this is how we do it'. And so we decided to start a workroom, and that is really the heart of what we do and it is

actively hands-on. We're engaged in making fashion every day, because unless you get inside it you can't know how it works and how to possibly do it differently.'

Since 2000, MATERIALBYPRODUCT has unfolded as a whisper rather than a grand statement in terms of its growth. For each person that has purchased a garment – be it a stylist, a curator or an intern from the workroom – another has asked them what they are wearing and become clients. Today, MATERIALBYPRODUCT caters predominantly to private clients around the world. This, according to the designers, changes the attitude of the studio, and although essentially it is a commercial venture, the approach is quite different to most businesses. Like a traditional European couture salon, MATERIALBYPRODUCT's creative space is a compact combination of

3 (From left) rubberised trench and jacket, S/S 08/09

'WE DON'T MAKE EXCUSES FOR FASHION BEING BUSINESS, AND IT DOESN'T HAVE TO BE ANY LESS CREDIBLE – INTELLECTUALLY, RIGOROUSLY OR CREATIVELY' – *Susan Dimasi*

studio, workroom and shopfront. 'It's our main centre of production and it all happens there. We invite a lot of people into the studio and we end up talking to people – business people, academics.' And although MATERIALBYPRODUCT found it challenging to create a house of this nature in Australia at the turn of the century, they were determined to foster a community that would surround and support it. 'When we started we positioned ourselves globally. We had a totally different modus operandi which has evolved into our business model. The culture has been generated by engaging people in the workroom. We've never been defined by a number of stockists.'

This concept has been appreciated by others, with MATERIALBYPRODUCT curated in gallery shows and their participation in the 080 Barcelona Fashion Week. As well as this, MATERIALBYPRODUCT received the Premier's Award for both commercial and cultural fashion design as part of the Melbourne Design Festival in both 2006 and 2008. The clothing itself ranges in style and form, from jackets and pants to floor-length dresses and tops. What sets it apart is its treatment or construction: embossed or laser-cut leather, prints, hardware, beading. The cut of each garment does not adhere to trend or tradition, but rather explores new ways of shaping the female form and subverting the purpose of the garment.

246

4 Rubberised curtain
dress, S/S 08/09

5 Still taken from film of
collection presentation at
080 Barcelona Fashion

6 Foil-printed screen
gown, A/W 09

NATHAN SMITH
NATHAN SMITH

Loose, relaxed and comfortable, Nathan Smith runs his business in a manner that reflects the style of his self-titled label. Smith's urban-style male and female collections suit Australia's laidback culture. The designer's beginnings on Sydney's northern beaches are inherent in his work, which remains inspired and influenced by its wearer.

Smith studied clothing production at a TAFE institute on New South Wales' north coast, learning here about patternmaking and manufacturing methods. Although not always interested in fashion, a younger Smith was surrounded by the industry from a very young age. His father the owner and director of a fashion group, Smith grew up 'writing swing tickets,' he tells. 'The family has been involved in fashion for as long as I can remember.' Following a brief stint in fashion retail, Smith opened his own independent clothing boutique, Cumquat, in Avalon, Sydney, when he was 22 years old. It was here that the Nathan Smith label was born.
'I had begun doing my own label whilst I was still working in and running the shop,' which remained open for almost three years under Smith's management and ownership. 'I started making t-shirts for the shop. The pieces were quite popular, and I began getting enquiries from other boutiques, so I guess it just went from there.'

Although the designer's work is now considerably recognised in the Australian fashion landscape, Smith still remains slightly outside industry regularity, choosing to create his own path, rather than follow that of someone else. Indeed, Nathan Smith is quite a niche brand, and is stocked only in several high-end stores around the country. This, he tells, is how it should remain. 'I am very happy with our current customer

'MY MOTHER WEARS IT, MY GIRLFRIEND WEARS IT, AND HOPEFULLY YOU'LL WEAR IT TOO'
– Nathan Smith

base domestically. I'm looking at working with our current stockists to expand the business.' By growing his business in such a manner, Smith allows himself the time and room to grow and 'learn as a designer and manufacturer.' The designer has chosen to wait until he has built stronger business infrastructure before considering an international launch. 'Ideally I'd love to show and sell overseas, like all designers.'

Smith reflects that his inspiration derives from a short attention span. 'No sooner have I finished one season and I'm already tired of it and onto the next. The tiredness of the last collection is inspiration enough to move onto the next.' The aesthetic, however, remains a constant. Described by Smith as 'simple, clean and comfortable,' the clothing, for both men and women, allows the wearer to play with and interchange styles with their mood or feeling. Typically drawing on a neutral, natural colour palette, Smith's use of cotton, wool and jersey is cut so that each garment seems a second skin to the wearer – at once comfortable and subtle. His signature style takes form in loosely shaped t-shirts, wrap-around cardigans, singlets,

1 Cotton voile skirt and cotton sarong, A/W 10

sarong-style ankle-length skirts and floor-length, scoop-necked dresses. Essentially, Smith's designs are basic enough for the wearer to pair them with other wardrobe items, allowing their personality to be expressed, and yet of high enough quality and with their own individual design quirks for them to be worn individually. It's perhaps for this reason that Smith believes his clothes are for everyone. 'I find that people who wear or buy the label aren't fanatical people. They appreciate the piece for what it is, and I don't think that this can be pigeonholed to a certain group or customer base. My mother wears it, my girlfriend wears it, and hopefully you'll wear it too.'

2 Cotton sarong and
t-shirt, A/W 10

3 Voile shirt and linen
pants, A/W 10

NICOLA FINETTI
NICOLA FINETTI

Having trained in architecture, it is little wonder that Nicola Finetti's womenswear collections have a strong tendency to be body-conscious each season. Varying in style, form, colour and pattern, Finetti's pieces consistently make a woman look and feel instantly sexy with their contouring shapes and use of complementary fabrics. According to Finetti, this is what he values the most in designing. 'I appreciate dressing women who have the courage to be different,' he tells. 'There is so much liberty to dressing that now, more than ever, women can express their individuality, femininity, invention and strength through my silhouettes and use of fabrics.'

Born and raised in Italy, and later living in Argentina, Finetti found his English-speaking skills to be 'less than fantastic' upon relocating to Australia, and so began expressing himself visually. A different industry to architecture – with different requirements and skills – fashion design provided Finetti with an outlet in which to communicate the way he envisioned the world and the people within it. And, as he tells, architectural knowledge forms very much a part of his work – there is 'so much structure in the clothes – they are very body-conscious.' However, it is in colour that Finetti finds the most inspiration, with each season reflecting an entirely different idea or attraction. 'It might be a colour that attracts me in a park or somewhere I am... or just people in the street. It could be a picture or a movie. The aesthetic, while body-conscious and strongly formed, is more related to colour, and we try to have a colour that has a very specific and unique tone and hue. Colour is the most important thing. It is the base of the collection.'

Indeed, the relationship between colour and form is one that defines the work of Nicola Finetti – bold, sensual and often daring. This dialogue is at once evident in Finetti's Spring/Summer 2008/2009 collection, which paired strong colour and precise, sharp tailoring to create dresses that seemed powerful and sensual. In mini lengths and with horizontally layered pleats, Finetti used a graduated tone of deep violet right through to white in a bandage dress, held together around the bust with a belt-like band, enveloping the woman in an hourglass silhouette. And while Finetti's signature style is always recognisable and present in his collections, he tells that the techniques used are 'always changing. Now, for example, we are doing something that is very 1980s, heavy in construction, with pieces applied to the garments. The concept is different each time.'

The Nicola Finetti brand forms the core of Finetti's business, which has grown since 1995 to include Nicola Finetti aXessory (2003), Nylon Flocks (2004), the Frisoni Finetti collaboration with Fernando Frisoni (2006) and, more recently, NF by Nicola Finetti for department store Myer. 'More or less,' Finetti tells, 'everything comes back to the same sort of style,' within the diffusion lines. 'Nylon Flocks was originally for the daughters of the mothers that were buying

1 Silk dress with sequined shoulders and jersey leggings, A/W 10

Nicola Finetti – it was younger and more affordable.' Although now a considerable size, Finetti still manages the business. 'It is one of the things you have to do. You have to see what is going on and what the image of the brand is for the public.' The aim for the imminent future is to grow on an international level, where Finetti believes the label has a lot of potential. 'And afterward,' he adds, 'I would like to do some collaborations. When we have a special project to work on the creativity is better.'

'COLOUR IS
THE MOST
IMPORTANT
THING. IT IS
THE BASE
OF THE
COLLECTION'
– Nicola Finetti

2 Silk satin dress, A/W 10.

NOM*D
MARGARITA ROBERTSON

Self-described as dark and wittily sombre, NOM*d is a quintessentially New Zealand fashion label. Headed by Margarita Robertson and husband Chris, the fashion business began over two decades ago, stemming from a small boutique in a back street of Dunedin in New Zealand's South Island. Today, NOM*d has a legion of followers worldwide, each vying for the utilitarian clothing that 'adopts the cool, considered gaze of the fashion outsider,' says Robertson. Just don't confuse the designer's penchant for black as a gothic reference: 'there is also humour and love of summer.'

'We started NOM*d in 1986, concentrating mainly on knitwear,' tells designer Margarita Roberston. With many contacts in the rag trade established through the existing boutique, Robertson found approaching retailers fairly easy. As she explains, 'they were ready for some unique and wearable designs.' The ease with which the business has grown is evident in the designs. Often androgynous and tough, each collection begins with 'a different starting point. Often the fabrics [direct] me towards a certain look, sometimes a movie... and we always reference our own ideas from past collections – it's important for our style to remain recognisable.' Such clothes are usually pre-washed and unironed, giving them a slightly worn-in feel and adding minor imperfections, which has come to be a hallmark of NOM*d design. Besides, 'perfection is boring!' quips Robertson.

Of Greek-Ukrainian background, Robertson was exposed to fabrics and patterns from an early age as her mother sewed clothes for her and her siblings. As a teenager, she began making her own clothes and became involved in the burgeoning fashion scene of the time. 'I was one of those dedicated followers of fashion of the 1960s', she says jokingly.

'I managed the business side of things from the beginning until around 1999', tells Robertson. From this point, financial administrators relieved the workload to allow for greater creative breathing space. Managing the business, Robertson gained strong experience ('I know exactly what money came and went, and what moves to make next') that has helped sustain a solid financial base for the company today. Promotional assistance for the label has been provided along the way, with the Trade and Enterprise and NZ Wools supporting NOM*d in showing at London Fashion Week in 1999, alongside three fellow NZ designers. The experience 'certainly gave us the encouragement to expose ourselves fully in the northern hemisphere and made us realise that we had a collection that stood up beside any of our northern counterparts.' The label has also shown at New Zealand Fashion Week on several occasions, proving an invaluable experience.

Still based in Dunedin, NZ, NOM*d is clearly influenced by the bare surroundings of the area, though Roberston believes that the collection is truly global, not specifically designed with

1 Textured wool sweater, A/W 08

New Zealand in mind. That said, Roberston is proud of the state of fashion in her home country: 'we are so fortunate in having consumers that expect high quality, upmarket brands to come out of New Zealand, because traditionally we have not been exposed to luxury fashion from Europe. For many labels like ourselves, our dedication to the local industry has paid off – I think it's alive and kicking!' Helping to maintain this growth and industry is NOM*d itself, not only with its broad reputation but manufacturing onshore with 20 staff in their studio. Roberston explains there are no plans to change this system in the future. Instead, NOM*d will 'continue to evolve as it has – aware of new ideas and developments and making carefully considered changes when necessary.'

2 Cotton wrap-around
waistcoat, cotton dress worn
over silk dress, S/S 09/10

3 Wool dress, A/W 08

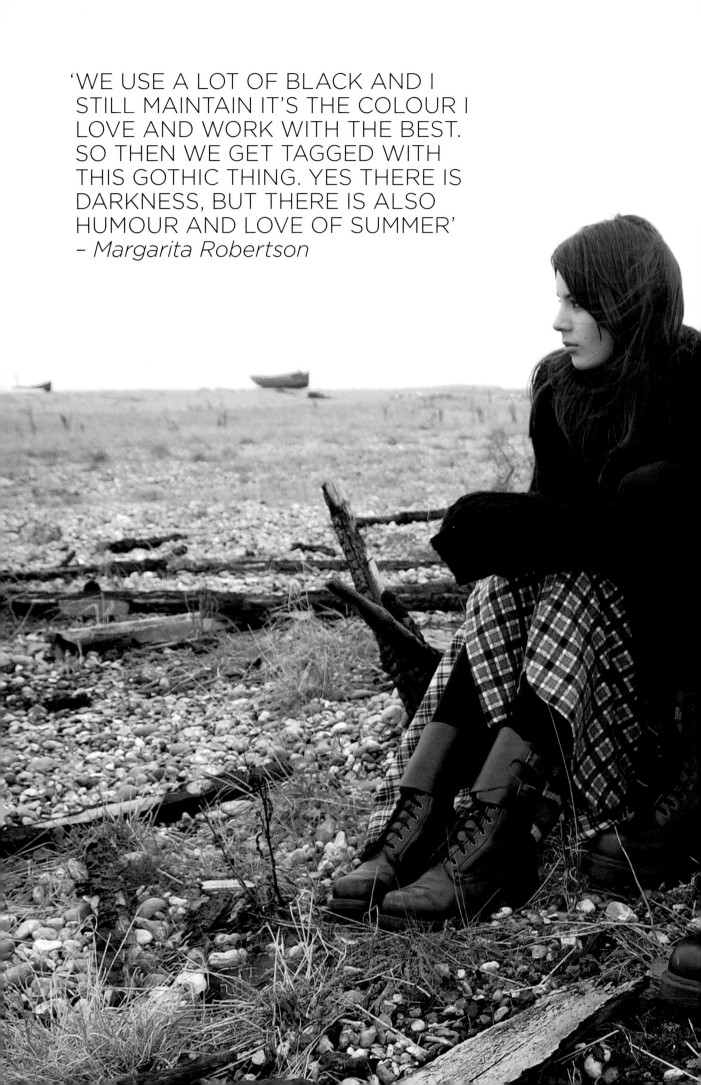

'WE USE A LOT OF BLACK AND I
STILL MAINTAIN IT'S THE COLOUR I
LOVE AND WORK WITH THE BEST.
SO THEN WE GET TAGGED WITH
THIS GOTHIC THING. YES THERE IS
DARKNESS, BUT THERE IS ALSO
HUMOUR AND LOVE OF SUMMER'
– Margarita Robertson

4 (From left) acrylic mohair sweater, wool cashmere pants and vintage flannel shirt; leather hooded jacket, acrylic mohair sweater and stretch drill pants, A/W 05

PERKS AND MINI [PAM]
MISHA HOLLENBACH
AND SHAUNA TOOHEY

Melbourne label Perks and Mini [PAM] is one of those indefinable creative entities that is involved in numerous artistic collaborations and left-of-centre ventures that blur the boundaries between fashion and art – a rare breed of designers whose creative energies vibrate further than the consumptive products of their labour. Headed by couple Misha Hollenbach and Shauna Toohey, PAM doesn't have a business plan and has never officially launched their work as expected by today's commercial market. And yet as a creative collective, PAM has one of the strongest international followings of any Australian fashion label, due in part to their constant assessment and reflection of the cultures that surround them.

Meeting in 1999 and marrying in 2000, Hollenbach and Toohey both have backgrounds in visual arts and graphics, and created the first PAM collection as pieces to take on their honeymoon. As Hollenbach explains, 'we still haven't 'launched' anything yet, or even done a business plan. We started very naturally and organically.' Despite the pair's obvious reservations about playing to the conceived and stereotyped notion of a fashion label, interest surrounded PAM and its products from the beginning – if not with artistic admiration, then out of curiosity. 'We have always been interested in the cultures that surround us,' note the pair in relation to their previous experience with fashion, creating an inextricable link between fashion and its social context. 'Dress-ups and costumes have always been a part of my life, even now. I guess this idea of clothing as a means of expression – in a creative, investigative way – hasn't allowed me to dismiss [fashion] as a valid art form,' says Hollenbach.

1 Cotton jersey t-shirt, viscose
scarf, cotton lycra leggings and
canvas bag, S/S 08/09

Art – most specifically graphics,
visual collaborations and books
– form the central root of PAM
and its values. 'Print, graphics and
images are super important to
PAM. Whether it be fabric, t-shirt,
embroidery, catalogue, magazine,
zine or hangtag... visual imagery
is a huge part of our overall
aesthetic.' Indeed, the designers
have collaborated with the likes of
illustrator Fontaine Anderson
for their Spring/Summer
2008/2009 *Space Face* collection.
'We collaborate because we share
feelings and energies that are
similar and like the idea of what will
come out of joining together,' the
pair explain. 'It's fun to work with
friends, and we have always had the
idea that two or three brains are
better than one!'

Described by the designers as
'spazzy and fun,' the clothes each
season communicate ideas of
psychedelia and imagination, yet
often reflect the world Hollenbach
and Toohey immerse themselves
in. 'The world is full of beautiful
things,' they note reassuringly.
'We are interested in everything
around us... those things that 'talk'
to us: interesting tastes, strange
objects, traditional cultures. We
are not interested in inspirations of
other fashion designers or artists;
sometimes we are into their work,
of course, but this would never be a
catalyst for our ideas. It's generally
an energy we pick up from [fellow]
creators.' PAM's mode of design
and research seems relative to
their style of work, which can't be
categorised in terms of genre or
style, but instead evokes a feeling
or image, and is designed for
'anyone that wants to get down!'

As well as clothing, Hollenbach
and Toohey manage a publishing
extension of their business,
PAMBooks, which allows them
to introduce and promote the
work of artists and friends.
'These [books] are furthering the
ideas of creativity, freedom and
communication.' Newly-released
publications include the work of
Albert Oehlen, Andora Wekua and
Mark Borthwick.

'WE HAVE ALWAYS BEEN INTERESTED IN THE CULTURES THAT SURROUND US'
– Misha Hollenbach

2 Nylon jacket, cotton jersey
t-shirt, polyester pants and
titanium sunglasses, S/S 08/09

In another extension of their clothing line, PAM opened a concession store within Japanese department store Parco in the Shibuya district. Spending three months designing the quirky fit-out and heightening their cult status in Japan, PAM had already reached fever pitch in response to their clothing and, more specifically, their playful shoes, accessories and jewellery. With hordes of followers overseas, it seems interesting that PAM remained – and still to a degree do remain – quite low-key in Australia. 'I think we are part of a global culture, something which the internet has allowed to happen in an exponential way,' says Hollenbach. 'This global idea was already obvious to us, and more so, this is how we are living. Travel and expanding horizons are so important to us.' This mode of growth is manageable as the pair still direct and administer the business, though they find it an 'absolute chore.' However, exponential growth is not the main objective in the PAM journey. Instead, the designers are developing a way to go 'deeper into our world', noting that graphics and shapes are becoming more intense and that they are exploring their practise further.

3 Polyester cape and polyester
satin hat, S/S 08/09

PISTOLS AT DAWN
ANDREW BYRNE AND JOSH McPHERSON

There is some confusion surrounding Brisbane-based label Pistols at Dawn. Not because the clothes themselves are confusing – it's high quality suiting and wardrobe staples – but because it forms only a part of the business established by friends Andrew Byrne and Josh McPherson. 'The Pistols [at Dawn] range is our creative arm,' explains McPherson. 'Producing a seasonal off-the-peg collection allows us to be involved with Mercedes-Benz Brisbane Fashion Festival and other projects.'

Parallel to this range, Byrne and McPherson offer a made-to-order suiting service that goes by the name of The Cloakroom, also the name of their Sydney and Brisbane stores. As McPherson continues, 'The Cloakroom is an in-house tailoring service, where you choose everything: the collar, the cuffs, have your name embroidered on the inside of your jacket. Out of necessity we started Pistols at Dawn so that someone can walk into the shop and buy something straight away.' And many have, if the duo's retail progression is anything to go by. Having opened their Brisbane store in 2007, The Cloakroom opened a boutique in a back street of Sydney's fashionable Surry Hills in 2009. In keeping with the laidback aesthetic of the clothes, many a customer has mistaken their entry to the shop as that of a bar. A dark timber bench acts as a counter, whilst the black concrete floors and walls create a cavernous atmosphere that perfectly frames the dusty-coloured collection that hangs subtly along the main wall.

'I'm not particularly confident with colour and pattern,' tells McPherson, 'and so what we offer is quite block in tone, which allows people to accessorise with watches, shoes and ties. What we design isn't flamboyant.' Which, for Australian men attempting to navigate the

1 & 2 Cotton blazer, S/S 08/09

bi-annual European trends, is a godsend. What's more is that the pieces are made with the Australian climate in mind, offering the perfect combination of wearability and relevance. 'It gets very hot, particularly in Brisbane, and so guys become averse to wearing jackets through the summer. We've employed the construction of half-lined jackets in lightweight wools and linens, and using soft-weight shoulder pads which are actually layers of canvas rather than stiff padding.' The Cloakroom stores have a full offering of accessories and shoes (they happen to be the local agent for Grenson, the classic English shoemaker), making it something of a one-stop-shop for the modern man's wardrobe.

While McPherson's background is furniture design, Byrne worked in the corporate sector and found himself making business shirts to-order for colleagues and friends who were looking for something different – better fitting, higher quality, more individual. Having studied together at university, Byrne and McPherson reunited several years later and decided to build upon the hobby business that Byrne had established. 'Our customer base from here opened up to a whole bunch of colleagues from the design world,' explains McPherson. 'The suits and pieces we make aren't typically corporate, so we gained quite a following for what we offer.' And, slowly and steadily, the duo is helping to change the existing perceptions of men's style in Australia.

3 Linen blazer, cotton shirt and polished cotton shorts, S/S 08/09

'WHAT WE DESIGN ISN'T FAMBOYANT. IT DOESN'T TRANSLATE TO A RUNWAY, AS SUCH'
– *Josh McPherson*

it's not the usual wardrobe option for an Australian male – but then, if they have the confidence, they'll end up wearing it and, hopefully, loving it.' The designers believe that the slow shift of attention to men's fashion is due to the likes of photographer/blogger Scott Schuman, better known as The Sartorialist, for fashion becoming increasingly accessible. '[The Sartorialist] is not just voyeuristic, but gives guys an opportunity to have a look and be inspired, even if they're not particularly into 'fashion'. When you see an older guy with salt-and-pepper hair, smoking a cigar and wearing a silk cravat with a double-breasted jacket... well that for any guy is inspiring, because that guy is real, he's got a real job. People can relate and aspire to that.'

McPherson and Byrne have told many who have entered the store looking for a suit: 'go and spend as much as you wanted to spend on a suit on a pair of new shoes, and then come and see us. You can make a $2000 suit look like a Lowes special with the wrong pair of shoes.'

Pistols at Dawn has shown at Mercedes-Benz Fashion Festival in Brisbane in 2008 and 2009 in group menswear shows.
As McPherson and Byrne explain, the range doesn't translate to a runway automatically. They've added simple accessories such as hats and sandals – accessories that are sold alongside the suiting in The Cloakroom. 'Guys off the street wonder for a bit whether they could pull off wearing a tailored jacket with shorts and a sandal – because

4 Cotton blazer,
cotton shirt and
linen trousers,
S/S 08/09

ROMANCE WAS BORN
ANNA PLUNKETT AND LUKE SALES

With a self-confessed love of kitsch Australiana, combined with a dynamic, thematic-based and crafty approach to design, Anna Plunkett and Luke Sales defy convention with their much-loved label Romance Was Born. Their lavishly theatrical collections and runway shows present a hybrid of outlandish ideas and concepts, drawn together by their unique ability to own trends rather than follow them.

Upon entering the Romance Was Born studio in Sydney, one could mistake their location for that of a children's art class. Most often there are people scattered across the floor, lending a creative hand to the designers – beading, gluing, plaiting, decorating – as they ramp up for another spectacular collection. Other times, there are people just hanging out – friends, interns, groupies and admirers. On the odd occasion you might even find artist Del Kathryn Barton, with whom the designers have collaborated with on prints. It's a busy place, and Plunkett and Sales wouldn't have it any other way. Just as their clothes are created from a fusion of fabrics and techniques, their vision is inspired by their creatively energised surroundings, and it shows in their clothes. In a multi-coloured, playful palette, Romance Was Born's aesthetic often includes a mix of appliqué, tie-dying and crochet, while their prints are derived from work with artist collaborations. Such a creative force by its very nature understandably attracts a keen following.

However Romance Was Born isn't out to exploit the talent of others. Plunkett and Sales have worked tirelessly since the birth of the label to sustain a commercial business. Having met whilst studying fashion at TAFE Design Institute, the designers became fast friends with the dream

1 Silk metal
dress, A/W 10

of creating a label together.
'I always liked making clothes and reading fashion magazines, but never felt confident enough to become a designer,' recalls Plunkett of her youth in NSW's country town of Albury. 'I knew of Luke at [TAFE], but we weren't friends at first and were in different classes. I saw his clothes backstage at a show and realised he was my only competition in the course.' Finding the projects in the course 'boring', the pair worked together to make the ride more exciting. One such exciting venture was approaching singer Karen O of Yeah Yeah Yeahs fame to dress her in a one-off creation for her 2003 Australian tour, and after viewing the pair's sketches, Karen O settled on a dazzling red tulle and lace halter-top that became a visual sensation. 'We really love her!' add the designers. Since this time, Romance Was Born has dressed many A-list performers, including Cyndi Lauper, Debbie Harry, Lily Allen and Bat for Lashes.

Upon graduating from fashion school, Plunkett and Sales were selected to attend the International Support Awards in Italy.
'That made us realise we could really do this,' explains Plunkett. 'It was a collection of one-offs and we thought 'this is pretty cool,' and we got offered several jobs, but it wasn't the right time and we wanted to come home and do our own thing.' One of the jobs to which they lightheartedly refer was an internship with John Galliano, which they famously turned down – reportedly one of the best decisions the designers ever made. Instead, the pair returned to Sydney where they 'started making clothes that people were interested in and [they] started buying them.'

2 Denim jeans and fleece
sweater, A/W 10

Now producing collections on a seasonal basis, Romance Was Born has gained recognition around the world, with a growing understanding that the pieces, while theatrical and daring, are also extremely wearable and accessible when broken down. 'I don't know where our inspiration comes from, though once we get talking about something for a while it just stays there and grows,' explain the pair. With their 2009 collection for Australian Fashion Week – aptly titled *Doilies and Pearls, Oysters and Shells* – the idea for an under-the-sea grandma-mermaid tea party was inspired by the classic Prince song *Diamonds and Pearls,* which played as one of the tracks in the fairytale show staged overlooking the water at Sydney Theatre Company. 'Luke and I think that if you're going to do a show, then put on a show!' exclaims Plunkett. 'A conventional runway doesn't inspire us. We design a full look and concept, and so our shows evoke emotion, just as the clothing should.' This particular collection was lauded as their best to date, not least for its spectacular staging, but in that it successfully and

harmoniously married their quirky eclecticism with classical tailoring and silhouettes.

Romance Was Born was awarded the New Designer Award in 2009, supported by Woolmark and presented by *Vogue* Australia, allowing the pair to experiment with and expand the use of wool in their work. For the designers, this rates as one of the ultimate highs in their rollercoaster career: 'just to be acknowledged by Woolmark – it's good to know we can be appreciated on that commercial level as well.' What they refer to, here, is the breaking down of their pieces. 'We like to think Romance Was Born has its own style or signature, with its own prints and cuts and shapes, and sometimes people find it hard to translate this when buying in a shop.' That said, the label is renowned and loved for pushing conventional boundaries and dazzling one-off creations. 'Our one-offs are on a different level – we don't call it couture, a piece might be made from garbage bags – but whatever we do comes back to what we are producing in our ready-to-wear.'

3 Silk jersey blazer, polyester spandex
bodysuit and wool pants, A/W 10

4 Collection presentation
at Australian Fashion
Week, S/S 09/10

'IT'S MORE OF A FEELING
THAN A LOOK'
– Anna Plunkett

SASS & BIDE
SARAH-JANE CLARKE AND HEIDI MIDDLETON

sass & bide is the brainchild of friends Sarah-Jane Clarke and Heidi Middleton. Launched in 1999 with innovative denim designs, the iconic Australian label – best known for its urban take on Australian glamour – expanded into seasonal ready-to-wear within two years of its inception. Under Clarke and Middleton's creative direction, sass & bide now operates three distinct ranges and maintains broad recognition and distribution internationally.

As Clarke tells, 'we share an innate fascination and curiosity for fashion,' which helps to explain her career transition from accountant to designer, whilst Middleton had worked as an advertising art director. When they decided to launch a label, explains Middleton, each had 'a big heart, empty pockets, and creative vision.' It's this singular vision – an unwavering objective to remain true to their personal style and artistic ideas – that has been the label's most potently successful aspect.
'We went headfirst with a collective obsession for clothes.' First selling their wares on London's Portobello Road, the designers' stretch jeans with two-inch zippers became a trend-setting hit worldwide, spurring the development of their main line. sass & bide followed this by showing at London Fashion Week in 2002 and later in Sydney and New York.

In an aesthetic the designers describe as 'a clash of the strong, the beautiful and the obscure,' sass & bide's signature ready-to-wear line is supplemented by S&B VIE, a younger, more accessible diffusion of the main line, as well as sass & bide denim, in the genre they were first and are still best known.

1 (From left) lace dress with leather straps; silk dress with mirror and bead embellishment, S/S 09/10

As the designers tell, inspiration is drawn from life beneath the surface 'right in front of you.' While each line varies in terms of price point, fabrication and trend, what is inherent throughout is the designers' signature hand: a combination of tribal, glamour, luxury, urban and surf elements that together create a distinct hybrid unique to sass & bide. While the designers' individual garments continually explore new ideas and concepts, from low-cut, long silk singlet-dresses to their black 'rat' leggings (which spurred an international trend phenomenon) the pair are perhaps best recognised for their quirky and exaggerated styling. Hardware, feathers and sequins often adorn simple dresses and tops, giving them a somewhat tribal, and definitely individual, appearance. And as Middleton explains, the customer for whom they design is 'an independent thinker with a free spirit and an appreciation of the beauty that surrounds her.' That sass & bide is occupied with and appreciative of natural beauty speaks lengths of the designers' integrity and ability to connect with women the world over. As the designers believe, 'kindness is more important than wisdom. We celebrate this virtue as our philosophy.'

In just a decade, sass & bide has grown considerably, and is available in high-end department stores throughout the world, as well as managing ten of its own stores in Australia, with plans for greater retail expansion in Europe. Clarke and Middleton direct 'all things creative,' hiring 'the best people to fill the gaps' in their demanding and continually growing business. To date, the designers have collaborated with British high-street department chain Topshop (in 2008 on a denim line) and Lovable, for which they design a lingerie range. Both collaborations are testament to the strength and recognition of the sass & bide label and aesthetic. Yet despite the growth, Clarke and Middleton remain humble about their success and realistic about their goals, noting their favourite fashion moment as their first show. 'It was fresh, uninhibited and we were surrounded by friends.'

'WE SHARE AN INNATE
FASCINATION AND
CURIOSITY FOR FASHION'
– Sarah-Jane Clark

'WE'VE HAD A CONSISTENT
VISION OF OUR AESTHETIC
FROM THE BEGINNING'
– *Gary Theodore*

3 Silk chiffon dress,
S/S 04/05

4 Silk twill jacket and silk
chiffon skirt, S/S 04/05

5 Silk and tulle dress and
cotton cardigan, S/S 04/05

SEVENTH WONDERLAND
BONNIE COUMBE

It is little wonder that Australia should be the world's swimwear capital, given our beach culture and long-running affinity with the water. And yet, as designer Bonnie Coumbe and her partner Carlos Aviles found, there lacks an established relationship between swimwear and fashion. In response to a market that consisted of only a few designers, together they created Seventh Wonderland for women who yearn for 'absolute quality in unique, functional and beautifully constructed swimwear, infused with a distinct look that embodies art, lifestyle and romance.'

Founded in the winter of 2008 after a long-running 'will we, won't we?' debate, Seventh Wonderland made its official debut at the acclaimed Miami Swim Fashion Week, a 'completely different world' for the pair. Application protocol for the event dictates that labels must be established for three years before they are even considered to exhibit at the trade fair that attracts buyers and press from around the globe and is considered to be the most prominent and revered showing of swimwear in the world. However, as Aviles tells, 'they took a risk on us because the committee liked our ideas. It's a really big deal because they usually only accept major international names.' The pair's support network for the event consisted of themselves and, as they found out, steadfast Australian swimwear label Zimmermann. 'It's interesting to see the Australian labels there,' adds Coumbe. 'Everyone sticks together.'

Launching a first collection in such an exposed and large-scale atmosphere as Miami is a recipe for failure. Undeterred, Coumbe and Aviles were not interested in doing anything on a small scale and wanted to 'do it right.' As Coumbe explains of the first season, 'we shocked them

1 Polyester elastane swimsuit, S/S 09/10

because we did this collection of black, silver and chrome, as opposed to bright prints that are usually expected. It was a way for us to really get ourselves out there.' And indeed this approach sparked interest from media and buyers, for Seventh Wonderland was invited back to the event the following year.

With a background in graphic and textile design, Coumbe brings to the label an attention to creative detail, which is evident in the hand-created prints, trims and the evolving silhouettes that promote stylish functionality. 'My grandma is a tailor and my mum is in textiles, so I learnt how to sew when I was about eight years old,' she explains. 'I still freelance today as a textile designer in Europe and the USA,'

says Coumbe, which includes prints for Karolina York. Coumbe's knowledge and skill creates new propositions in the typically staid swimwear industry, and Seventh Wonderland proudly injects personality to its swimwear with the use of fashion techniques such as bead work, smocking and pleating, and using hand-dyed Italian fabrics. As Coumbe tells, 'with Seventh Wonderland, it is all about technique and detailing, because there is no point coming out with just another swimwear label. We want to make it fashionable.'

Coumbe's partner Aviles manages the business from a branding point of view, including marketing, advertising and image concept. Together, the pair created Seventh Wonderland to fulfil their joint

2 Polyester elastane
swimsuit, S/S 08/09

'I CREATE ALL
OF THE PRINTS
BY HAND,
WHICH HAS
BECOME MY
SIGNATURE
IN A WAY'
– *Bonnie Coumbe*

desire of creating their own label. 'We deliberated for nearly two years,' says Coumbe. As her textile work was being purchased by an increasing number of design houses, they together decided to 'do it, and set about creating an amazing first collection.' And so Coumbe and Aviles established a brand with a distinct aesthetic and business practice that they describe as their own expression. 'What we do gets people thinking about swimwear. We push the boundaries in developing shapes, and with limited fabric space you have to think outside the square and be creative to present new ideas each season. There are so many ways of wearing it that differ from the traditional.' Chosen fabric, too, is unusual. As well as being hand-designed and dyed, Seventh Wonderland only use a recently developed environmentally-friendly fabric that doesn't tear or snag, allowing them to experiment with techniques such as laser-cutting.

Continuing to show at Miami, and having been apart of the first IMG Australian Swim Week, Coumbe and Aviles are focused on developing their swimwear while simultaneously introducing outerwear ('cover-ups you can put on over the top'). 'We just want to get this right and then move onto the next thing. It's about longevity.' And while they believe Australian swimwear is really evolving, they believe there is still much room to grow, both locally and internationally. 'Australia is starting to support its own labels and creativity.'

3 Polyester elastane
swimsuit, S/S 08/09

SOMETHING ELSE
NATALIE WOOD

Like its namesake, Something Else is an outlet for its designer Natalie Wood to combine creative disciplines. As she collaborates on each collection with respected artists, the strength of the brand lies in the merging of art and fashion. Previously the creative director of womenswear for the globally recognised surf brand Insight, Wood was the founder of cult label Sample and of art project Beauty of Nature before launching Something in 2004, which became Something Else in 2006.

A culmination of high fashion and street edge – designed, according to Wood, 'for girls who are experimental with their style' – Something Else has found a niche in the international market, with stockists spread across the globe. Wood is, as she tells, 'quite surprised about winding up in fashion.' The designer studied fashion design at RMIT Univeristy, where she 'took all and any courses available to give myself much experience and training, including life drawing and art classes.' As a teenager Wood was heavily involved in various music scenes, which resulted in her attaining a very individual look that she created herself. 'I saw the fusion of a subculture and fashion at this time,' she adds. Working in retail also gave Wood a greater understanding of how and why people buy clothes. However, the greatest experience came for Wood when her former partner created a custom-printed t-shirt label. 'The process of collaboration and creation gave me my first real insight into the world of commercial fashion design,' she recalls. 'It was my first foray into creating an actual brand.'

Wood's experience was based on the idea of 'something growing organically', which she preferred as a method of development as it allowed for an emphasis on the creative process. Wood next created Sample in collaboration with Vanessa Coyle, which was a collection of 'super high-end garments with amazing creativity.' As Wood tells, from that point on 'the journey has been quite insane.' Indeed, following the success of Sample, Wood assumed her role at Insight. 'It was here,' she tells 'that I learned the true value of the commercial marketplace... through my involvement with the brand, a new market was forged.' What Wood refers to here is the way she shaped Insight into more of a fashion-conscious label with full creative attention. 'It was a really magical journey with Insight, and I learnt so much about the development of a large commercial brand and business. It was certainly wild to see something you helped create go on to be so internationally successful.'

Throughout her various creative ventures, Wood noticed a 'rather large' gap in the market for something more conceptual, art-based or one-off. 'This prompted the initial concept of Something,' she tells. 'I really tested the waters, developing the label and its identity quite slowly. After the label got to a certain point, I added a higher-end line [in 2006] and made an

1 Silk crepe dress, A/W 10

official launch at Australian Fashion Week,' with what is today known as Something Else. And just as Wood intends her clothes to bring artistic ideas to life, her first show involved building a life sized doll's house, which 'really showed my need for fusing fashion with art – something that is very dear to my heart.'

Something Else has continually collaborated with artists from various creative disciplines, including Georgina Cullum, Deanne Cheuk, Michaela Saunders, Skullux, Fontaine Anderson and Tara Marynowsky. It is this blend of an artist's vision and Wood's ability to interpret it into something tangible, wearable and accessible that gives Something Else its strength.

'I YEARN FOR A SENSE
OF SPIRITUALITY TO BE
PRESENT IN MY WORK,
GIVING THE WEARER
AN ETHEREAL SENSE
OF THE LOVE POURED
INTO EACH GARMENT'
– *Natalie Wood*

And Something Else isn't typically categorised as an 'art brand', a term applied to those few avant garde designers that create distinctly unwearable, yet aesthetically phenomenal, collections. Instead, the unique work of Wood and her team results in a form of streetwear, for lack of a better word, inspired by music, culture and visual arts. 'Generally I have only one style rule,' says Wood, 'and that is to keep everything looking effortless.' True to Wood's aim, Something Else collections rely heavily on the use of layering and oversized garments ('everything keeps getting bigger and bigger'), in both width and length, allowing the fabric to wrap, mould and drape itself around the wearer. 'And yet, a certain tomboyish feel can be contrasted with a soft, feminine style, too. I love beautiful fabrics and exquisite cuts. The emphasis is always on comfort.' That Wood interacts and collaborates with artists to create clothing collections is both rare or commendable, but is secondary to her intention to keep these inherently wearable, comfortable and true to the artist's creative idea. 'Art is really important to me in my creative process, and I really see clothing as a kind of mobile canvas. I have always treated the artwork as being precious and special as something you might hang on your wall. The process of collaborating with artists really is so exciting.' Perhaps Wood's most prevalent collaborator is Georgina Cullum. 'We have a really innate understanding of each other and the Something Else aesthetic. I value our beautiful working relationship to no end. It's true to say that the artists I work with are the exact people I have in mind when I design. This is the market I design for.' If Wood's success is any indication, then it's fair to say that a market for her work definitely exists. 'She is a really creative, artistic, stylish girl that is confident in herself,' Wood says of her customer. And while the designer feels that her label is well-recognised in the local market, there is room for growth internationally. Something Else maintains sales agents throughout Asia, New Zealand, the USA, Canada and Europe. 'The strategy has been based around making good collections, placing them in the right stores and having the product speak for itself and sell well. Our business has grown through great sell through as opposed to a heavy marketing plan.' Business is something that Wood has kept an eye on personally, learning, along the way, to trust her 'gut instinct on things. Decisions should never be made solely based on money.' In this vein, Wood's goal is to 'stay positive by believing in and loving what [we] are doing.'

2 Modal elastane dress,
leggings, bag and scarf, and
cotton knit cardigan, A/W 10

THERESE RAWSTHORNE
THERESE RAWSTHORNE

'I don't have an ultimate goal in terms of something I wake up with each morning and set out to achieve,' says renowned Australian designer Therese Rawsthorne. 'For me, fashion is a real journey and a progression each season. If you get to your destination then it's over for you.'

Rawsthorne was raised in an isolated area and was interested in fashion as a teenager but didn't realise an industry existed with employment opportunities. When finally she did discover a new world, the designer's charm and talent led her to work with the inimitable Issey Miyake and Ozwald Boateng, returning to Sydney in 2003, where she launched her own label under the name of Youth World. 'It was so inspiring working with Issey – he has a childlike playfulness that makes you realise it doesn't matter what age you are or where you are from, you can achieve your dreams.' Starting out in her bedroom producing very small collections and working three part-time jobs, Rawsthorne managed to book some appointments with buyers in her first season, and built her label from there.

After three years trading as Youth World, Rawsthorne was forced to re-brand her label under her own name due to a conflict of naming rights which prevented her from selling to the American market. Continuing to grow her business, the designer has shown her collections at Australian Fashion Week, believing the event to be 'a great platform to get your name out there and show your stuff.' Rawsthorne has received much support from the media in her few years as a designer in Australia, including her first season at Australian Fashion Week when 'an editor flew into the room with sunglasses and scarves flying and assistants trailing after; I thought she might have been lost and so I introduced myself and

1 Coated linen jacket with print from collaboration with Linda Jackson, silk top with polyester trim, and coated linen skirt, S/S 09/10

she knew who I was – she was there to see me and my work!'

Rawsthorne's natural design approach has created a sophisticated aesthetic with clean lines, attention to detail and luxurious finishes. Inspired by movies, books and imagery that she finds along the way, the designer explains that the process of creating a collection 'is quite research-driven.' Before beginning in her design studio, Rawsthorne spends time gathering references and ideas that come to influence the style and form of each collection. Singlehandedly running and managing her business, Rawsthorne caters to a woman who is complex and multi-faceted and wants to wear clothes that

'are versatile and not fad-driven.' In most of her collections is a slight tomboy element, presented with femininity and subtlety. While Rawsthorne designs with a woman in mind, the clothes don't overpower a personality or individual style. Most often this is in the form of fashion staples: collared white shirts, tailored pants, light cotton summer shirt dresses, and classically tailored yet slouchy blazers. By combining traditions of fabric and cut with modern stylistic elements, Rawsthorne's signature hand is evident in the evolving dialogue of her work.

2 Silk dress and
cotton slip, S/S 09/10

'DESIGN IS DRIVEN BY CURIOSITY AND
THE SEARCH FOR SOMETHING NEW'
– *Therese Rawsthorne*

3 Coated linen jacket with print from
collaboration with Linda Jackson, silk
top with polyester trim, and coated
linen skirt, S/S 09/10

THREE OVER ONE
JIM THOMPSON

It's rare in a world of mass production to find a fashion label that prides itself on producing high-quality, hard-working clothes. Inspired by the integrity of 1940s post-war design, Jim Thompson established Three Over One to complete the working man's wardrobe. In doing so, Thompson has filled a large gap in the international men's market, offering stylish, quality clothes that last, season upon season.

'That we produce and throw away doesn't sit well with me. The luxury market is fine when there is quality attached, but I had become very disillusioned by the industry and the idea of mass consumerism and poor quality,' explains Thompson. Having worked in the industry for years as a buyer and product developer, Thompson had trouble finding clothes he wanted to wear, and so instead invested in a lot of vintage pieces found on his international travels. It is here, in his favourite design era of the 1940s, that Thompson discovered true quality that appealed to him. 'The workmanship is something that you don't see much today,' he adds.

Three Over One, despite its clear design vision and philosophy, was created in early 2009 as an extension of Thompson's fashion branding and production business. The Spring/Summer 2009/2010 season was the first publicly accessible, finding stockists in 10 stores throughout Australia, though the label had already garnered much interest with its inherently unique design perspective that resonated with the economic climate of the time. 'That positive outlook of the future during the 1940s – after a war and a heavy depression – might be a similar situation to today,' muses Thompson on the apparent success of his first season. Managing all aspects of the business during its early stages, the designer is

FRANK HOODED SWEAT

1 Cotton hooded sweater and wool track shorts, A/W 10

well-qualified in the field of brand building and production, with broad industry experience from high end through to mass-market labels. 'Fashion was something I wanted to do from a really young age. I went in the direction of business and marketing, studying at the University of Manchester in England, and then working in manufacturing and business before moving to Australia.' Designing by himself may be new to Thompson, but his influences and creative ideal seems strong enough to lead him through any problems.

'I always wanted to do something that I truly believed in and something that I wanted to wear.

Design in Australia is very safe, and falls between two camps: the younger, fashion group and the more mature, preppy labels that try to fill the gap. There wasn't anything that represented the crossover between the youth market and a more vintage look.' And indeed, people agree, with support from Thompson's venture coming from media, buyers and the consumer. 'People want to get behind new things and champion new designers.' Thompson launched his label in a time of great economic insecurity, and he found the process of selling his collection tough. However the range was received well by stores and during its first season was being courted by retailers in the UK and USA. 'I want to ensure I keep it to a certain size rather than anything too large-scale,' notes Thompson, wanting instead to maintain the label's niche offering in the market.

2 Cotton shirt, vest
and pants, A/W 10

WILLIAM WAISTCOAT
CHARLIE TWINPLEAT TROUSER

JACK TRACK SHORT
HENRY TRACK PANT

3 Cotton hooded sweater, wool track
shorts and cotton track pants, A/W 10

WALTER DENIM TROUSERS
3/ ONE   D29.42

4 Cotton shirt and
denim jeans, A/W 10

'I LOOK TO AN ERA
THAT'S ABOUT THE
QUALITY, PURPOSE AND
FUNCTIONALITY
OF THE LABEL. IT'S
ABOUT GETTING BACK
TO THAT INTEGRITY
OF WORKMANSHIP OF
CLOTHES THAT PEOPLE
CAN WEAR SEASON IN
AND SEASON OUT'
– *Jim Thompson*

JOSEPH WORKERS COA   3/ ONE   D29.42

TOMMY WORK SHIRT
HERBERT DENIM

5 Wool coat, A/W 10

TINA KALIVAS

TINA KALIVAS

Tina Kalivas is one of Australia's unabashed masters of construction. Having trained with some of the world's most revered designers, Kalivas combines her experience in costume design and haute couture with structurally conceptual clothes that capture the zeitgeist.

As Kalivas recalls, fashion was always something she dreamt of doing. 'I made clothes for my stuffed animals as a child, and although I entertained the idea of pursuing other careers, it's the only thing I was quite good at.' Interestingly, Kalivas studied period underwear and corsetry at the London College of Fashion, providing a grounding in construction that would remain inherent in her work for years to come. This experience was furthered as she worked under the tutelage of British designers including Clements Ribeiro, Russell Sage and, most notably, the late Alexander McQueen: as an experience, she tells, it 'was wonderful. I really enjoyed working on the showpieces and bringing his eccentric ideas to life.' And although people often describe Kalivas' clothing as having European influences, this exists not so much in the styling or fabrication, but in the ways in which her designs are executed – with knowledge, precision and attention to detail.

In a similar vein, Kalivas also worked – and continues to do so sporadically – as the costume designer in cinema, most recently the Japanese film *Goemon* (2009). This, she believes, has a strong influence on her work. 'It adds another angle to the way I construct and realise the clothes that are in my mind.' The designer's work is inspired by ethnicity, nature and outer space. 'I love documentaries and enjoy adding an 'other worldly' edge to each collection.' Such an aesthetic Kalivas describes as 'arty

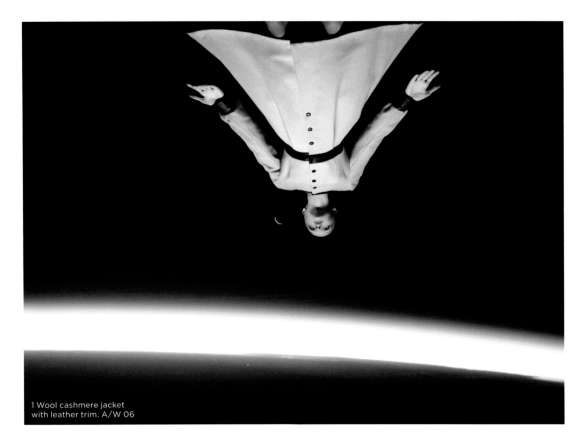

1 Wool cashmere jacket
with leather trim, A/W 06

and structured but organic,'
created through the use of an
extensive range of techniques.
Evident in each collection is
specially created and dyed prints,
appliqué, embroidery and knits, all
of which evolve in a 'diverse and
experimental process.' In achieving
distinct and unique form, Kalivas
uses historical references inherent
in the cut of her clothes, which
she sculpts and drapes on the
mannequin. A double-layered
mini-skirt – the under layer in
straight-cut, bandage style, and
the upper a ballooning peplum
of ruffles – held together with
an ethnic-printed waist band is
evidence of such combinations.
From the same collection is a
cotton shift dress that subverts
perception through its play on
structure, the middle of the
garment forming the centre of an

origami creation, with pleats, folds
and layers distorting the use of the
print to create something visually
dynamic, like a Rubik's cube that
isn't yet complete.

Kalivas launched her label in 2002,
creating the first collection herself
on a single sewing machine. 'I put a
bit of promotional material together
and then the right people came on
board to guide me and help out
with press and sales.' Today, Kalivas
is stocked throughout Australasia,
United Kingdom and Dubai. Kalivas'
customer base – which is, as she
tells, an extremely wide range of
people – is far flung around the
world. 'I am constantly amazed by
the people who buy my clothes.
Many people tell me they have 'this
great jacket' that will never go out
of fashion because it's unique, and
that really makes me so happy,

2 Patent leather
jacket, S/S 09/10

whoever they are. My favourite moments are when I see girls out looking
and feeling fantastic in my clothes. This is the ultimate achievement.'

Testament to Kalivas' popularity and expertise, the designer has created
specially-commissioned collections for high street retailer Kookai and
the uniforms for the Hilton Hotel, each to great acclaim and in keeping
with her usual wit and design flair. As Kalivas tells, 'I let things evolve
organically and find that opportunities present themselves and lead
you into new directions. I like to remain open minded about the future
and concentrate on the present moment.'

3 Silk georgette
dress, A/W 06

4 Wool jersey
dress, A/W 06

'FASHION IS ALWAYS
A DIVERSE AND
EXPERIMENTAL PROCESS'
– *Tina Kalivas*

5 Tie-dyed wool dress
with silk tulle and metallic
embroidery, S/S 09/10

6 Tie-dyed silk
dress, S/S 09/10

TONI MATICEVSKI
TONI MATICEVSKI

'Fashion has been milked in too many ways. There are too many festivals and events and footballers and rooftop underwear shows and all that shit. It's really draining and people really aren't that stupid,' says Toni Maticevski of the Australian fashion industry. Instead of staging publicity stunts or seeking media attention, Maticevski has dedicated himself to his art. Over a decade after launching his own label, the designer is praised internationally for his work that has been described as 'demi couture'.

Raised in Melbourne, Maticevski studied fashion design at RMIT University, graduating with first-class honours. Winning the Fashion Group International Award upon graduating, Maticevski was honoured with a period of work placement with Donna Karan in New York where he was offered a full-time position. Finding the large house creatively draining, the designer moved to Paris and worked for Cerruti before returning to Melbourne to launch his own label in 1998. As he tells, 'it happened really quietly and before I knew it I was designing collections every season.'

Finding inspiration in music, Maticevski designs emotively to create elaborate gowns and separates that embody a sense of fluidity. Each season is a continuation of dialogue from the previous, reacting to both the climate and the wearer in an alluring, foreign language. Indeed, Maticevski's work is the antithesis of 21st century fast fashion. 'I love using beautiful fabrics and having quality finishing in my work and subtle details that make clothes special,' he says. His work often plays with varying ideas of texture and technique, combining materials such as fur and sequins – those which can elsewhere come across as tackily theatrical, but here do not – in ways that enhance and empower a woman's figure.

His statement pieces, often worn by celebrities, are as delicate as they are spectacular, with fine laces, draped chiffon and metallic embellishments. Couture is defined by the Chambre Syndicale as being based in Paris with a workshop of at least 15 staff – but if Australia can claim to have haute couture designers, Toni Maticevski is one of few. His contribution to the local industry – international interest, inspiration and a unique offering – is of immeasurable importance.

Maticevski's aesthetic and modus operandi have been well received by the industry, winning him the Best New Designer award at the Melbourne Fashion Festival in 2002 and the Prix de Marie Claire Best New Designer award in 2005. Part of the Australian infiltration of New York in 2006, Maticevski showed his collection at New York Fashion Week alongside six fellow antipodeans including sass & bide and Ksubi. 'It just feels like a natural progression to move forward and go to other places,' he explains of the choice to continue showing abroad. 'I love New York!' In a celebratory homecoming, Maticevski staged a show in 2009 that presented his favourite pieces from 10 years of archived work, those which didn't fit individually in other collections. The show was a godsend – a gift to Australian fashion in a time of reduction and bleak outlook.

Maticevski shies away from talking about the development of his label, claiming that 'it is never good to talk about things you are going to do… you just end up with egg on your face.' Maticevski is however deeply involved with the business side of things, believing it is imperative to understand and know everything to keep on top of it. While not letting on about future business plans, he is quick to affirm that his work shall continue 'for a long time. I love to work with people from wherever, as long as they like to work with me.'

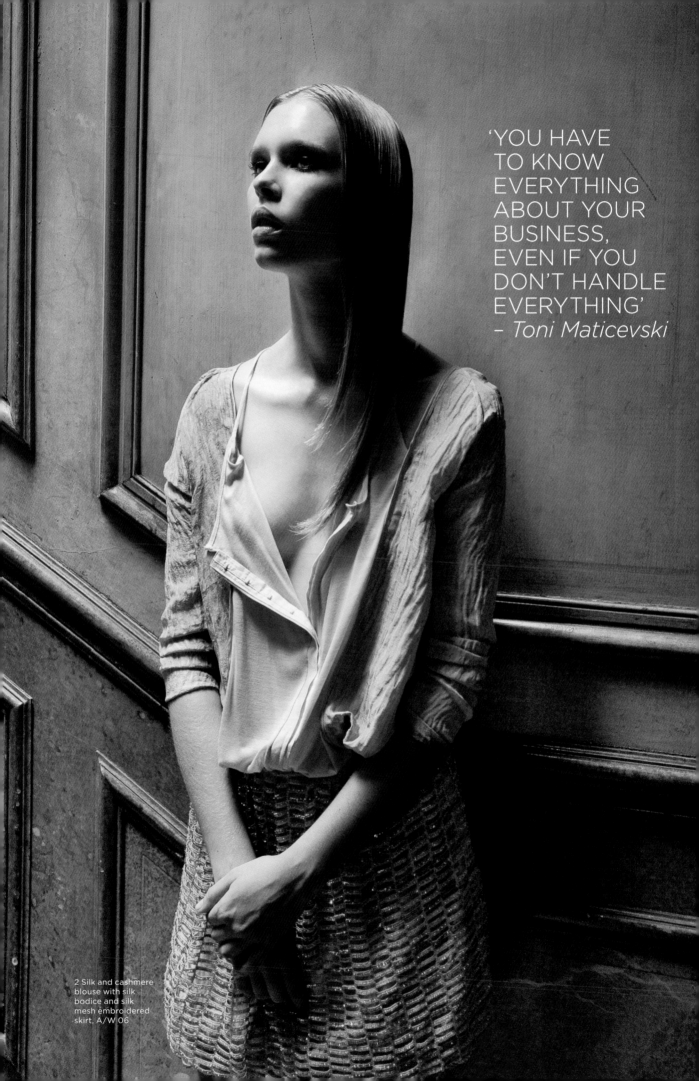

'YOU HAVE
TO KNOW
EVERYTHING
ABOUT YOUR
BUSINESS,
EVEN IF YOU
DON'T HANDLE
EVERYTHING'
– *Toni Maticevski*

2 Silk and cashmere
blouse with silk
bodice and silk
mesh embroidered
skirt, A/W 06

3 Cotton jersey and
double-layered silk
dress, A/W 06

4 Printed silk dress with
silk organza bodice and
twisted jersey seam
detailing, A/W '06

TV

MONIKA TYWANEK
AND INGRID VERNER

Melbourne-based label TV provide a complex mode of conversation through their cult-followed collections. Rejecting balance in favour of concentrated focus on a singular idea, the TV aesthetic is bold and uncompromising, and yet simultaneously tongue-in-cheek with a fair dose of wit. Produced collaboratively by Ingrid Verner and Monika Tywanek, TV's unique approach to the art of dressing is a refreshing addition to the Australian industry and one with an international following.

Verner and Tywanek met whilst studying fashion and textiles, respectively, at RMIT University, and formed their intuitive partnership in their final year of study. 'We worked on our first collection during my fourth year at RMIT,' explains Verner. 'We collaborated from there and launched the label the following year at the Melbourne Fashion Festival.' It was in this first season at the festival that Verner and Tywanek were awarded the Tiffany & Co. Designer Award for their debut collection. In its initial stages of development, and even still today, the designers found varied support in the Australian fashion industry. According to Verner, 'the press are very supportive. With buyers, some are, but they do not take risks in the buying itself. What is lacking is what we see in other countries where the government and independent sponsors actively support the fashion industry by way of substantial and ongoing fashion grants and awards.' Australia is, however, a relatively young country compared to its European counterparts with established fashion houses, larger populations and historically-steeped fashion industries. On a domestic level, TV has found Australian Fashion Week as the most relevant and important event for their brand.

The future of TV, according to the designers, is in the international market, working with a wholesale agency to expand their activity throughout Europe. For TV to function as a sustainable business, it seems fitting that the designers should broaden their outlook overseas. While the clothes are wearable and well-constructed, there lies something of a thought process in the way in which the style is put together.

Inspired by the natural world of textures, colours and shapes, the 'constant theme across each TV collection is the interplay between my designs and Monika's expertise in textile development,' tells Verner. 'Sometimes in pushing the boundaries of taste, re-interpretation and in the search for new combinations.' This combination, they tell, creates an aesthetic that lies somewhere playful between Kate Bush, Linda Jackson and Neneh Cherry. 'It is elegance imbued with a wry sense of humour,' she adds, 'exploiting its Australian roots without falling for the cheap clichés of cringe.' And, as per the designer's apt description, TV collections do indeed employ the use of varying and contrasting techniques and ideas, weaved together in creation

1 Silk and cotton jersey dress and stretch jersey shorts, S/S 08/09

of textural knits that accentuate the form, or shifting shapes that are brought to life through innovative fabric treatments. Perhaps their most iconic piece is a cloth-draped dress that, when displayed with extended arms, showcases a square cut pattern that spells TV. 'It's about clever construction and modern cutting techniques composed in innovative layers and textures.' This, they tell, is for 'confident girls, adventurous women and a few crazy boys.'

Verner and Tywanek together manage both the business and creative development of their label, which proves 'a real challenge but potentially a very rewarding one,' according to Verner. 'Balancing the creative with the business side is our focus for the future.'

2 Hand-painted cotton
patchwork jacket, cotton
dress and hand-painted
cotton bum-bag, S/S 08/09

'WE ARE UNDERSTANDING MORE AND MORE
THE IMPORTANCE OF, AND OPPORTUNITIES
IN, BEING POSITIONED INTERNATIONALLY'
– *Ingrid Verner*

3 Silk shorts, hand-painted
silk tank, mesh leggings and
hand-knitted cotton jersey
bag, S/S 08/09

VANISHING ELEPHANT
HUW BENNETT, FELIX CHAN AND ARRAN RUSSELL

With a name stemming from a quirky short story by Haruki Murakami, Vanishing Elephant is a label of distinctly refined, classic menswear. Made up of Huw Bennett , Felix Chan and Arran Russell, the young label is growing at a steady rate as it caters to an international market in an economic climate that has seen a return to classic dressing.

It's a return, according to the trio, that has been a long time coming. 'We're quite different to Australian menswear brands in that our collection is really based around shirting,' says Chan. 'It has always been like that and will remain like that. We try to be quite classic, as that whole androgynous, layered look is not what we like or what we wear.' As Bennett continues, 'We are all classic, easy dressing guys, and so steer clear of trends as much as possible. Our collections often come out looking quite collegiate in style, but we touch on that workwear aesthetic by using some harder colours. We're finding there is a return to classic clothing, anyway. At the end of the day we're not reinventing the wheel. It's a matter of making pieces that are classic and work well. While our colours are quite seasonal, the silhouettes remain very classic and timeless.' They believe, too, that people have embraced their brand because it is cleaner and easier to understand than many others. 'Having a coloured woven shirt and a pair of chinos is quite classic,' says Bennett, explaining the appeal of their simple and stylish range.

The designers candidly state that they don't have, and have no intention of creating, a bold statement or innovation through their clothes. This is in keeping with their realistic view of the market and their place within it, which is perhaps a result of their combined experience in fashion sales,

1 Cotton jersey
shirt and cotton
knit sweater,
A/W 10

marketing, design and production.
Chan and Bennett, sales agents,
together established the brand
in 2008, soon after bringing on
board third member Russell, who
had previously managed his own
label (Martial Artist). 'It was a
pretty natural step for all of us,'
believes Chan. 'We had known
each other for quite a while and
we all recognised the gap in the
menswear market.' Though,
as Bennett adds, 'it wasn't one of
those things that we sat down and
thought "ok, there is a big gap,
so we're going to make X, Y and
Z". There was just an opportunity
there, and it all came about by
chance, really. And we've had
a good response and been really
happy with it.'

The thrust of the brand, aesthetic
aside, is its accessibility and price
point. 'That, for us, is a really big
thing,' says Chan. The designers
are adamant that their products
should be available at a price

'WE'RE NOT REINVENTING THE WHEEL. IT'S A MATTER OF MAKING PIECES THAT ARE CLASSIC AND WORK WELL'
– Huw Bennett

point akin to fast fashion, such as Britain's Topshop, but without the market saturation. 'We want to make it affordable to the everyday customer. We don't want people to gawk at our prices,' adds Russell. Vanishing Elephant is stocked in 20 boutiques domestically, and has sales agents and distributors in all corners of the world, though the international market has developed more slowly than the southern hemisphere. 'It's the nature of the beast,' says Bennett. 'If we were in America, then America would be our strongest selling location.' As well as boutique stockists, Vanishing Elephant is stocked by General Pants Co. Australia wide, which has provided the burgeoning label a strong, broad platform in which to present itself. 'It limits your boutique business [being stocked in a chain store],' explains Bennett, 'but we really sit on that line [between] fast, accessible fashion and boutique brand.' The three believe that the future of the brand is not to saturate the market, but to build a presence within existing retailers, which will filter through in sales. 'It's a hard thing to balance, but we need to support the people that support us,' says Chan.

The creation of each collection begins collaboratively with the trio, working from an initial theme, translating this into a mood board, and then sketching ideas, shapes and silhouettes. From this point, Russell, with a design and production background, creates line drawings and then travels to China to deal directly with their manufacturers. 'I've been working with the same factories for 10 years and they're really great,' says Russell. 'A lot of people are anti-China when it comes to production, but they're really helpful and the quality is amazing! They really do a better job than anyone else and are happy to experiment with new techniques.' Vanishing Elephant has a considerably large distribution base, and have built a reputation by consistently delivering their classically stylish collections on time each season.

2 Cotton shirt, wool and
cotton knit waistcoat and
wool pants, A/W 10

WILLOW
KIT WILLOW

Launching in 2003 with a lingerie collection, WILLOW has evolved into a fully-rounded and developed clothing label recognised for its easy and approachable interpretation of high-end luxury. Today the WILLOW name is synonymous with Australian fashion, as is fitting for a label that resonates with the needs of Australian women.

WILLOW's founder and designer, Kit Willow, says fashion has always been a firm focus for her. 'I was obsessed with theatre and fashion from three years old. Just born with fashion obsessions.' Although Willow completed tertiary education at Melbourne's Monash University majoring in marketing and philosophy, fashion remained a central hobby. Creating clothes out of old scarves, which she would sell from a stall on High Street in Melbourne's Armadale, Willow got her break working with high-end boutique store Georges, in Melbourne, and later at Witchery, before establishing WILLOW. 'I jumped in the deep end, as I always do, and launched at Australian Fashion Week,' she explains. 'I could not believe just how supportive everyone was after launching the label. Before I launched, though, it was very difficult getting anything from suppliers and finding the right team.' Showing at Australian Fashion Week, however, provided the fledgling designer with a 'wonderful platform' upon which to expand her label into fashion. This growth is mirrored in the designer's development and continued exploration of boundaries and new concepts, earning her an international reputation.

The designer describes her clothing as 'classics with a design twist. They are just beautiful, wearable pieces – always refined and always balanced in aesthetic – for strong, hard-working women of the world.' Known for

1 Beaded silk dress,
A/W 09

combining luxurious silks, wools and soft leathers, Willow has forged a niche in the Australian market for the pure simplicity and elegance of her work. As she tells, inspiration is found in nature, which seems fitting given the organic elegance of each garment. More specifically, the designer looks at flow, form and colour, providing her with a starting point for each garment, be it a structured wool zip-up jacket or a softly flowing dress with fragmented ruffles. Corsetry is an area that she returns to time and time again, drawing on her earlier years designing lingerie. 'I love working with fabric and allowing it to tell me where to go. I drape and work on the stand with fabric a lot. Tailoring and perfecting armhole and shoulder shape and ease of movement is very important. I also love laser-cutting edges to allow fabric to finish as it pleases, not stressing it with double turns. I also like working with clever artists to develop interesting textiles.'

In 2007, 2008 and 2010 WILLOW showed its collection at New York Fashion Week, helping to establish an international market and audience for the label. As Willow tells, showing in New York helps immeasurably. 'It definitely pushes me as a designer to create the WILLOW look – a look that embraces original ideas and yet is competitive on an international level.' The flow-on from this activity is evident in the growth of WILLOW in the UK and US markets. Domestically, WILLOW maintains three branded boutiques in Melbourne and another in Sydney. 'Retail in Australia is very encouraging and very satisfying in terms of displaying product in an environment that speaks the brand.' Willow manages the creative vision and direction of her label, providing the opportunity to express ideas each season in an unrestrained and uninhibited manner.

It's important, the designer believes, for creativity to be at the forefront of her agenda. 'I want to enjoy every moment and constantly evolve perfect techniques and design, and continually satisfy our customer,' she tells honestly. 'Fashion creates experience in people's lives. To add and enhance that is what it comes down to.'

2 (From left) silk dress and wool and feather capelet; cotton jacket, silk dress and leather boots; silk top, metal-beaded polyester skirt and elastic and metal-beaded necklace; silk dress, polyester scarf and leather belt; cotton and viscose jacket and polyester scarf, A/W 09

'I WANT TO
KEEP ENJOYING
THE DESIGN
PROCESS'
– *Yeojin Bae*

4 Silk skirt and top, S/S 08/09

ZAMBESI
ELISABETH FINDLAY

With a singular design vision and unwavering aesthetic, Zambesi has
forged a reputation as one of New Zealand's strongest and most global
fashion labels. Epitomising the individual spirit, both the women's and
men's lines of the brand 'redefine convention with an ironic practicality',
reflective of the imaginative spirit of designer Elisabeth Findlay's
home country.

Findlay had opened a multi-branded fashion boutique in 1975 before
establishing Zambesi with husband Neville in 1979. Zambesi is also one of
the oldest labels in existence in the New Zealand market. The key to such
enduring success, believes Findlay, is having a holistic view of the business.
'I had completed a commercial course at school, and subsequently
worked in an office for several years which equipped me with a basic
understanding of business and administration. Neville also has a solid
understanding of the business, and the rest is just common sense.'
Indeed, the business itself has been built to support the artistic vision
of Findlay, as opposed to creativity supporting commerce.
Opening their first flagship store in Auckland in 1982, several other
concept stores have opened in New Zealand as well as Sydney and
Melbourne, 'creating the desired environment to present the collections,'
explains Findlay. 'The stores reflect the brand's philosophy and give our
customers a further understanding of our identity.'

The Zambesi aesthetic is strongly identifiable. Working from and inspired
by fabrics, Findlay notes that the isolation and freedom of the New
Zealand landscape plays a great part in all aspects of the country's
creative fields. To support this culture, Zambesi employs its 50 staff

1 Cotton shirt and nylon trench, S/S 09/10

members in Auckland, where it also manufactures the vast majority of its products. With the ideal customer in mind – 'a person who looks beyond fashion trends and is interested in developing their own personal style' – Findlay uses traditional methods of tailoring and cutting to create strong, dynamic collections using varying combinations of shapes and cuts with a mixture of fabrics and colours, predominantly in a dark or neutral palette. 'It's intuitive and instinctive,' explains Findlay. 'We strive to achieve a high standard of workmanship.' This aesthetic and method of work is echoed in Zambesi's menswear range, designed by Dayne Johnston, but rather offers a masculine interpretation of Zambesi's design values and philosophy. 'It conveys a modern attitude and influence,' adds Findlay.

Zambesi has shown regularly as part of both Australian Fashion Week and New Zealand Fashion Week, as well as part of the New Zealand Four Collection at London Fashion Week in 1999. Such events are used by Zambesi to 'present the collection in the full, desired aesthetic.' As well as this, Findlay believes, such events are important to the industry, for both new and established designers to springboard their evolving brand ideas. For Zambesi, the high number of students visiting their workroom attests the growing enthusiasm for the rag trade. Having recently celebrated three decades in the industry, it is no wonder so many students and fellow designers alike salute and celebrate Zambesi's success. Humbly, Findlay believes 'there is still much potential in the brand,' looking forward to the future.

'I HAVE ALWAYS WORKED INSTINCTIVELY FROM THE FABRIC TO CREATE THE DESIGN. I WORK FROM AN ARCHIVE OF FABRICS COLLECTED OVER THE YEARS WHICH I AM ALWAYS ADDING TO AND USING WHEN THE MOOD TAKES ME'
– *Elisabeth Findlay*

2 Cotton dress and wool gloves, A/W 08

3 Cotton tank, rayon
jacket and cotton
jeans, S/S 08/09

ZIMMERMANN
NICKY AND SIMONE ZIMMERMANN

Beginning as a start-up at Sydney's Paddington markets in 1991, Zimmermann is now recognised as one of the most iconic swimwear labels in the world. Sisters Nicky and Simone Zimmermann today manage the business and design each range as a feminine and sexy reflection of Sydney beach life. Dynamic and strong, each piece of their collection has a distinctly recognisable aspect of Zimmermann's history and story within it.

It makes sense that a swimwear business should hold the crown as one of Australia's most successful and globally recognised fashion designers, for Australia is known for its beaches and swim culture. But despite this, Zimmermann has respectfully earned its place in Australia's burgeoning fashion industry, staying true to their values and creating in an innovative, fashion-forward manner. As such, Zimmermann can truly be referred to as 'fashion' as opposed to just swimwear. Indeed, their range now includes ready-to-wear and accessories that build upon the aesthetic and styles produced in the swim collections, creating a fully-rounded, complete wardrobe suitable for any warm climate.

While Simone is responsible for managing the operational aspects of the business – which has grown to include stores in Sydney, Melbourne, Adelaide, Brisbane and Surfers Paradise and a growing wholesale network in some of the world's most revered department stores – Nicky focuses on the design of the various collections. Trained in fashion design by the TAFE Design Institute, Nicky recalls wanting to design and make clothes from a very early age. 'I always played with fabric and made things, developing it into garments as I got older. In my early teens I would use my mum's sewing machine to make clothes for myself,' she explains. Upon

1 Nylon Lycra bikini, S/S 07/08

graduating from design school, Nicky worked in a range of hands-on design and production roles before beginning Zimmermann six months later, slowly developing a business around her popular and innovative swimwear. At this time, the concept of Australian fashion was still considered a paradox. 'You had to be self-sufficient and find a way to make a mark. There wasn't the attention on fashion, and no fashion week or sponsors or industry groups to advise you on a way to bring your label to life.' While Nicky believes this has changed in the years since her entry into the industry, she notes that the 'business of running a label is very difficult.'

In almost two decades, Zimmermann has experienced considerable success in its growth and recognition. Showing occasionally at Miami Swim Fashion Week, and with showrooms in Sydney, Melbourne, London and New York, Zimmermann also shows regularly at Australian Fashion Week, which they believe 'has evolved into a great event. We don't necessarily participate to secure international stockists – we are more focused on presenting our vision for the season to the local media and to support our Australian business, including our

retail and wholesale accounts.' In doing so, Zimmermann taper their approach to the Australian and international markets in different ways that respond to their presence in each. The overriding element, however, is a desire for continual success, not in way of sales but in design. 'We are trying to be better creators and I am trying to become a better designer,' says Nicky. 'We are all working harder and harder to do great collections, both in ready-to-wear and swim.' That said, Nicky believes she and her team work harder now than they ever have before, motivated by the design process and exploring new projects.

2 Silk dress,
A/W 10

'WE ARE TRYING
TO BE BETTER
CREATORS AND
I AM TRYING TO
BECOME A BETTER
DESIGNER'
– *Nicky Zimmermann*

3 Polyamide knit dress,
A/W 10

4 Nylon Lycra
bikini, S/S 07/08

DESIGNER CONTACTS

AKIRA
www.akira.com.au
+61 2 9557 0436

ALICE McCALL
www.alicemccall.com
+61 2 9280 0333

ALPHA60
www.alpha60.com.au
+61 3 9416 4296

ANNA & BOY
www.annaandboy.com
+61 2 9211 8511

ANT!PODIUM
www.antipodium.com
+61 8 9336 3925

ARNSDORF
www.arnsdorf.com.au
+61 3 9699 7604

AURELIO COSTARELLA
www.aureliocostarella.com
+61 8 9227 6535

BASSIKE
www.bassike.com
+61 2 9974 2664

BEAT POËT
www.beatpoet.net
+61 2 9380 9488

BETTINA LIANO
www.bettinaliano.com.au
+61 3 9539 5100

BIRTHDAY SUIT
www.birthdaysuit.com.au
+61 2 9331 6252

BRENT WILSON
www.brentwilson.com.au
+61 2 9283 2339

CAMILLA AND MARC
www.camillaandmarc.com
+61 2 9368 7711

CARL KAPP
www.carlkapp.com
+61 2 9331 5325

CHRØNICLES ØF NEVER
www.chroniclesofnever.com
+61 2 9280 0080

COLLETTE DINNIGAN
www.collettedinnigan.com.au
+61 2 8354 6426

CYBÈLE
www.cybele.co.nz
+64 9 365 1340

DHINI
www.dhinicouture.com
+61 3 9859 9810

DION LEE
www.dionlee.com
+61 2 9368 7711

EASTON PEARSON
www.eastonpearson.com
+61 7 3216 1649

ELLERY
www.elleryland.com
+61 2 9360 9100

ELSOM
www.elsom.com.au
+61 2 9011 7490

FERNANDO FRISONI
www.fernandofrisoni.com
+61 2 9360 9100

FLAMINGO SANDS
www.flamingosands.com
+61 3 9517 6535

FLEUR WOOD
www.fleurwood.com
+61 2 9380 9511

FRIEDRICH GRAY
www.friedrichgray.com
+61 2 8335 4503

GAIL SORRONDA
www.gailsorronda.com
+61 2 9380 9488

GARY BIGENI
www.garybigeni.com
+61 2 9380 9488

GINGER&SMART
www.gingerandsmart.com
+61 2 9380 9966

GORMAN
www.gorman.ws
+61 3 9429 0000

HOTEL BONDI SWIM
www.hotelbondiswim.com
+61 2 8399 2988

J'ATON COUTURE
www.jatoncouture.com
+61 3 9533 8666

JAYSON BRUNSDON
www.jaysonbrunsdon.com
+61 2 9698 2301

JIMMY D
www.jimmyd.co.nz
+64 9 379 8930

JONATHAN WARD
www.jonathanward.com.au,
www.rmwilliams.com.au
1800 339 532

JOSH GOOT
www.joshgoot.com
+61 2 8399 0533

KAREN WALKER
www.karenwalker.com
+64 9 361 0780

KARLA ŠPETIĆ
www.karlaspetic.com
+61 2 9380 9488

KATE SYLVESTER
www.katesylvester.com
+64 9 846 5225

KIRRILY JOHNSTON
www.kirrilyjohnston.com
+61 2 9282 9413

KONSTANTINA MITTAS
www.konstantinamittas.com
+61 2 9310 2225

KSUBI
www.ksubi.com
+61 2 8303 1400

LEONA EDMISTON
www.leonaedmiston.com
+61 2 9331 7177

LIFEWITHBIRD
www.lifewithbird.com
+61 3 9410 4580

LISA HO
www.lisaho.com
+61 2 8303 7888

LOVER
www.loverthelabel.com
+61 2 9699 2237

MANNING CARTELL
www.manningcartell.com
+61 2 9368 7711

MARNIE SKILLINGS
www.marnieskillings.com.au
+61 2 9369 1791

MATERIALBYPRODUCT
www.materialbyproduct.com
+61 3 9077 4796

NATHAN SMITH
www.thisisnathansmith.com
+61 2 8060 3006

NICOLA FINETTI
www.nicolafinetti.com
+61 2 9698 6497

NOM*D
www.nomd.co.nz
+64 3 477 7490

PERKS AND MINI
www.perksandmini.com
+61 3 9429 5211

PISTOLS AT DAWN
www.pistolsatdawn.com.au
+61 7 3210 1515

ROMANCE WAS BORN
www.romancewasborn.com
+61 2 9332 1114

SASS & BIDE
www.sassandbide.com
+61 2 9667 1667

SCANLAN & THEODORE
www.scanlantheodore.com.au
+61 3 9826 5742

SEVENTH WONDERLAND
www.seventhwonderland.com
+61 2 9360 7077

SOMETHING ELSE
www.something.net.au
+61 2 9380 9488

THERESE RAWSTHORNE
www.thereserawsthorne.com
+61 2 8084 0300

THREE OVER ONE
www.threeoverone.com
+61 2 9360 3609

TINA KALIVAS
www.tinakalivas.com
+61 2 9331 6252

TONI MATICEVSKI
www.tonimaticevski.com
+61 2 9356 2711

TV
www.tvthelabel.com
+61 3 9005 9391

VANISHING ELEPHANT
www.vanishingelephant.com
+61 2 9698 1688

WILLOW
www.willowltd.com
+61 2 9281 7355

WORLD
www.worldbrand.co.nz
+64 9 366 1555

YEOJIN BAE
www.yeojinbaedesign.com
+61 3 9529 2250

ZAMBESI
www.zambesi.co.nz
+64 9 308 0180

ZIMMERMANN
www.zimmermannwear.com
1800 738 895

PHOTOGRAPHY CREDITS

INTRODUCTION 1 Tanja Bruckner; 2-3 Georges Antoni; 4 Nick Hudson; 5-6 Simon Lekias. **AKIRA** 1-3 Stephen Ward. **ALICE McCALL** 1, 6-8 Pierre Toussaint; 2, 3, 5 Kane Skennar, 4 Alice McCall. **ALPHA60** 1 Lucas Dawson; 2 Six6 Photography; 3 Paul Barbera; 4 Alpha60; 5 Deb McFadzean. **ANNA & BOY** 1-2, 5 Jordan Graham; 3 David Mandelberg; 4 James Mullins. **ANT!PODiUM** 1 Geoffrey J. Finch, 2 Orangetoast, 3-4 Jonas Bresnan. **ARNSDORF** 1-6 Rene Vaile. **AURELIO COSTARELLA** 1-4, 7 Fabrizio Lipari; 5-6 Hamish Ta-mé. **BASSIKE** 1-4 Beau Grealy. **BEAT POËT** 1, 3-4 Glen Allsop; 2 Edward Bertouch. **BETTINA LIANO** 1-2, 4 Paul Empson; 3 Pierre Toussaint. **BIRTHDAY SUIT** 1-4 Liz Ham. **BRENT WILSON** 1-4 Anthony Geernaert. **CAMILLA AND MARC** 1-5 Bec Parsons. **CARL KAPP** 1, 3 Jez Smith; 2, 6 Carl Kapp; 4-5 Paul Empson. **CHRØNICLES ØF NEVER** 1-6 Scott Lowe; 7-8 Jeff Yiu. **COLLETTE DINNIGAN** 1-3 Ellen von Unwerth. **CYBÈLE** 1-3 Olivia Hemus. **DHINI** 1-4 Trevor King. **DION LEE** 1-8 Nick Hudson. **EASTON PEARSON** 1-3 Brad Hicks, Six6 Photography. **ELLERY** 1-3 Holly Blake. **ELSOM** 1-4 Ujin Lee. **FERNANDO FRISONI** 1-3 Adrian Mesko. **FLAMINGO SANDS** 1-3 Kane Skennar. **FLEUR WOOD** 1-3 Jordan Graham. **FRIEDRICH GRAY** 1, 4-5 Jordan Graham; 2 Scrapwall; 3 Orangetoast. **GAIL SORRONDA** 1-4 Amber Toms. **GARY BIGENI** 1-4 Rupert Tapper. **GINGER&SMART** 1-4, 6-7 Patrick McGreal; 5 David Mandelberg . **GORMAN** 1, 3 Ben Glezer; 2 Jesse Marlow. **HOTEL BONDI SWIM** 1-3 Derek Henderson. **J'ATON COUTURE** 1 Jez Smith; 2-3 Justin Smith. **JAYSON BRUNSDON** 1-5 Carlotta Moye. **JIMMY D** 1 Sam Crawford; 2 James Dobson; 3 Russ Flatt. **JONATHAN WARD** 1 Chris Colls; 2 Nick Leary. **JOSH GOOT** 1-6 Simon Lekias. **KAREN WALKER** 1, 3-5 Mikhail Gherman; 2 Derek Henderson. **KARLA ŠPETIĆ** 1-4 Rene Vaile. **KATE SYLVESTER** 1-5 Wayne Conway. **KIRRILY JOHNSTON** 1-2 Anthony Lau; 3 Bec Howell. **KONSTANTINA MITTAS** 1-3 Lyn Balzer and Tony Perkins. **KSUBI** 1 Lyn Balzer and Tony Perkins; 2-3 Liz Ham. **LEONA EDMISTON** 1-3 Ujin Lee. **LIFEWITHBIRD** 1-2 Steven Chee. **LISA HO** 1-3 Liz Ham. **LOVER** 1-4 Steven Chee. **MANNING CARTELL** 1-3 Steven Chee. **MARNIE SKILLINGS** 1-3 Mick Bruzzese. **MATERIALBYPRODUCT** 1-2 Rowan Dinning; 3-4 Susan Grdunac; 5 video still ; 6 Jeff Busloy. **NATHAN SMITH** 1-3 Kane Skennar. **NICOLA FINETTI** 1-3 Eddy Ming. **NOM*D** 1-4 Amy Troost. **PERKS AND MINI** 1-3 Tim and Barry. **PISTOLS AT DAWN** 1-4 Clare & Papi. **ROMANCE WAS BORN** 1-3 Tanja Bruckner; 4 Lucas Dawson. **SASS & BIDE** 1-2 Heidi Middleton. **SCANLAN & THEODORE** 1-5 David Armstrong. **SEVENTH WONDERLAND** 1 Tanja Bruckner; 2-3 Liz Ham. **SOMETHING ELSE** 1-2 Pierre Toussaint. **THERESE RAWSTHORNE** 1-3 Rene Vaile. **THREE OVER ONE** 1-5 Gerrard Needham. **TINA KALIVAS** 1, 3-4 Don Cameron; 2, 5-6 Larnce Gold. **TONI MATICEVSKI** 1-4 Jean-Francois Campos. **TV** 1-3 Kane Skennar. **VANISHING ELEPHANT** 1-2 Patrick McGreal. **WILLOW** 1-2 David Mandelberg. **WORLD** 1-3 Michael Ng. **YEOJIN BAE** 1, 3 Kane Skennar; 2, 4 Liz Ham. **ZAMBESI** 1-3 Marissa Findlay; 4 Javier Zalazar. **ZIMMERMANN** 1-4 Simon Lekias.

ACKNOWLEDGEMENTS

This book would not have been possible without the help and support of many talented and dedicated people.

Firstly, a big thank you to all of the designers involved, each of whom graciously allowed me an interview. Without such inspiring designers in Australia and New Zealand I would not have had the energy nor the resources to write such a book. To those creative people – photographers, stylists, art directors, models, and hair and make-up artists – who have supplied spectacular imagery, may this book in itself be thanks for your contribution to the artistic world. Many thanks must also be directed to the public relations professionals who have assisted me from the very beginning, particularly EVH, Golightly, Little Hero and M&P.

From concept to product, I thank you with the greatest of wishes: Paulina de Laveaux and Peter Shaw at Thames & Hudson Australia. May I also express my sincere gratitude to Melinda Crimp for her meticulous copy-editing and Allyson Crimp for the fantastic design of this book.

Lastly, to my friends and family who have dealt with my social absence and constant advice-seeking over the past two years, particularly Samuel Hodge, Elliott Wilshier, Jessica Beatson and Jolyon Mason.